E. McKnight Kauffer

Mark Haworth-Booth

E. McKnight Kauffer

a designer and his public

Gordon Fraser   London 1979

First published 1979 by
The Gordon Fraser Gallery Ltd, London and Bedford
Copyright © Mark Haworth-Booth 1979

British Library Cataloguing in Publication Data
  Haworth-Booth, Mark
  E. McKnight Kauffer
  I. Kauffer, E McKnight
  I. Kauffer, E McKnight
  769' .92'4   NCI850,K/

  ISBN 0 86092 034 8

Printed in Great Britain by Balding and Mansell, Wisbech
Bound by G & J Kitcat Ltd, London
Designed by Peter Guy

Contents

List of illustrations

The illustrations are reproduced by the kind courtesy of owners and/or copyright holders. Unless otherwise stated works are by Kauffer, and unless otherwise stated works are in the collection of the Victoria and Albert Museum.

List of Plates

Introduction

I first saw Kauffer's name on a poster while I was waiting for a train at Charing Cross Underground station in the summer of 1966. London Transport had reissued his 'Great Fire' poster of 1922 to mark the tercentenary of the Great Fire of London. It was evidently a poster of real attracting power (see plate 5) and I craned forward to find the artist's name. I read the curious legend 'E. McK. Kauffer' for the first time, and the date, '22'. I was doubly amazed – first that I had never before heard the name of this clearly remarkable painter/designer; second that his avant-garde design had been commissioned so long ago by a public utility company, the Underground Electric Railways Co of London. How? Why? About a year later I came across Kauffer again when his superb design of flying birds (on the title page and plate 4 of this book) was used on the jacket of E.H. Gombrich's book *Art and Illusion*. How fortunate to encounter Kauffer for the first time in his natural element – as an attention-grabbing but also wonderfully original designer, on a hoarding and on a book.

I began to find out a little about him – that he was American, that he came to England as a painter in 1914, found clients like the Underground who were promoting a new kind of advertising, that he was one of the most famous poster designers of his day, that he had returned to America in the last war. First I wanted to know when and why he had changed from painter to designer – later I wanted to know the beginning of the story in his native Montana and to hear what happened to him when he returned to New York in 1940. Who were the clients who made his adventurous career possible? How? Why? Since first coming across him by accident, every scrap of information I have found has been for me at least a startling new discovery, a shining new *fact* illuminating the mysterious (and by the 1960s and 70s already obscure) E. McK. Kauffer. Now that the book is finished, my ideal reader may well be someone whose interest in Kauffer began in a similar way. 'How?' 'Why?' However, the main value of the book will, I hope, be to provide a choice of Kauffer's work in reproduction and to win him new admirers.

The sub-title of the book, 'a designer and his public', is intended to emphasize Kauffer's relationship with his clients and critics, and to stress his own special view of the designer's role as an individual serving the public rather than exploiting it. Introducing the work of a young American designer, Paul Rand, in 1947 Kauffer wrote:

Like all good designers, his respect for the public is one of co-operation. The public really becomes the individual and the designer in turn, becomes the public – in the deeper meaning of the designer's thoughtful translation: his communication.
(Introduction to *Thoughts on Design* by Paul Rand)

The book is partly biographical because I think that Kauffer's career cannot be understood without knowing what he was like – the tenor of his mind as well as what he believed. I hope that by taking this biographical approach something may have been done for designers in general, who are usually patronized by art historians as the lower functionaries (like photographers until very recently) of some unreal Art World reserved apparently for 'real artists' like painters and so on. So far as I know this book is the first study of the life and work of a modern poster artist/designer. The pattern of neglect this involves is curious when set beside a prediction made in 1905 by H.P. Berlage:

On the basis of present social and artistic evolution: one will soon observe an interest in the growing body of useful arts, and a yearly decrease in the number of easel paintings and statues.
(Quoted by P. Reyner Banham, *Theory and Design in the First Machine Age*, p. 144).

Kauffer can be seen as a representative of a generation of artists who abandoned traditional media in favour of a wider, or more direct, social role. A group spread over many countries fulfilled Berlage's prophecy, including the classic photo-journalists like Henri Cartier-Bresson and Bill Brandt, and designers of the calibre of A.M. Cassandre, Jean Carlu, Ben Shahn and Herbert Bayer. Kauffer can be seen as a 'primitive' in the evolution of the new profession of graphic design. In this field as in others, the primitives remain perhaps the purest and the best.

The book is dedicated to the memory of G. McK. K., E. McK. K. and E. H-B.

Acknowledgements

This book does not cover the whole context of Kauffer's work and readers are advised to consult books by Martin Battersby and Bevis Hillier on international developments in the twenties and thirties: Bevis Hillier was the first to notice the Japanese model of Kauffer's famous *Flight* design, which remains the most fascinating stylistic discovery made about him. The British context of Kauffer's work has recently been deepened by Pat Gilmour's *Artists at Curwen* (1977), Christian Barman's biography of Frank Pick, *The Man Who Built London Transport*, (1979) and by the encyclopaedic Victoria and Albert Museum/Arts Council of Great Britain exhibition catalogue *Thirties: British art and design before the war* (1979).

I should like to thank Kauffer's family and friends for all the help they have so generously given me in preparing this book. In particular, Kauffer's daughter Ann Rendall, her husband Peter, and son Simon Rendall, have through their friendship and advice given me much help of all kinds. Mr Bernard Waldman of New York City and his daughter Grace Schulman have also been exceptionally kind and helpful, as has Mr Sidney Garrad in London. In preparing the checklist of Kauffer's published work, printed at the end of the book, I have been fortunate enough to have the co-operation of two Kauffer specialists, Dr Richard P. Wunder (formerly of the Cooper-Hewitt Museum of Design in New York) and Mr Alan Howell in London. I should like to thank Professor Giles Robertson and Dr Duncan McMillan of the University of Edinburgh for encouraging my initial work, Anthony Bell, John Taylor and Dr Herbert Spencer of Lund Humphries Ltd for furthering it, and Dr Alan M. Fern of the Library of Congress, Washington, and Mrs Elaine Dee of the Cooper-Hewitt Museum, New York, for their generous help in the United States. Kauffer's friends have remained devoted to him during the 25 years since his death and I should like to thank all of them and in particular Lord Clark, Sir Colin Anderson, Lord Bernstein, Lord Hutchinson, Lord Moyne, Lady Ashton, Lady Robinson, Mrs Jeanette Rutherston Powell, Colonel Frederick Beddington, Mrs Christopher Lobb, Mrs Mary Monkhouse, Mrs S.B. Webster, Miss Mary Blair Zimmern, Mrs Grevis Duce, Sir John Betjeman, Mr Paul Rand, Mr S.J. Perelman, Mr T.M. Heron, Mr Patrick Heron, Mr Whitney Straight, Major Charles Cousland, Mr W. Hellicar, Miss Jane B. Drew, Mr Theyre Lee-Elliott, Mrs Rosemary Pepler, Mrs Irene Wellington, and Dr Robert Leslie. Friends of Kauffer's, now dead, who gave much help were the late Maria Zimmern Petrie, Mr R.A. Bevan, Sir Francis Meynell RDI, Ashley Havinden RDI, Hans Schleger RDI, and Man Ray. I should also like to pay tribute to two great poster buffs – the late Osborne Robinson and the late Alan Mabey. I am most grateful to all those who have agreed to reproduction of illustrations or texts in their keeping, particularly Mrs Valerie Eliot. Friends and colleagues who have read the text at various points of completion, whom I should like to thank here for their advice are Peter Banham, Bill Feaver, Carol Hogben, Andrew Dempsey, Peter Howard, James Fraser, Gavin Graveson, my father, and Rosie my wife. My colleagues Sarah Woodcock and Philip Dyer of the Theatre Museum, and Valerie Mendes of the Department of Textiles have been unsparing providers of information, as have Michael Levey of London Transport, Philip Jaques of Shell, and Peyton Skipwith of the Fine Art Society. For encouragement at a time when publication of the book seemed impossible I am grateful to Dr Roy Strong and Dr Michael Kauffmann. My thanks also to Amy Bedik who was the main supplier of photographs for the book, including new prints from Kauffer's own negatives, and David Wright who has been, as always, an invaluable colleague. Finally, my warm appreciation is due to Gordon Fraser for his personal interest in the book and to Peter Guy, Michèle Mason, Judith Bastin and Averil Ashfield for their prompt and sure attention to all aspects of the editing and making of it.

Mark Haworth-Booth
Department of Prints, Drawings and Photographs
Victoria and Albert Museum

The Californian 1915 Painting by Maxwell Armfield

Chapter 1. **The Californian**

EDWARD KAUFFER was born in Great Falls, Cascade County, Montana on 14 December 1890, the only son of John and Anna Kauffer. His parents were both first generation immigrants to the United States, his father of Hanseatic German stock, his mother Swedish. John Kauffer was better known as Johnny Kifer, his professional name as violinist and trap-drummer with the Beach and Bower Minstrels and various show-boat bands. Edward Kauffer resembled his grandfather on the Kauffer side in hair and build.[1] A friend who met him in his early twenties described him as 'a very tall, lanky, good-looking man, with a slightly curved nose, blue eyes, a shock of red hair and the very light complexion that often goes with red hair'.[2]

Kauffer grew up in the small brewing town of Evansville on the Ohio River in Indiana, where the Kauffer grandparents had settled. Johnny Kifer was away for long periods with touring bands and the marriage was unsuccessful, ending in divorce when the child was three. As his mother was obliged to go out to work the boy was placed in an orphanage for two years. As a man of 60 he recalled with distaste the 'clipped hair, uniforms and impersonal dormitory methods'.[3] He grew up solitary and reflective in temperament, 'very much to myself always'. Like other children of poor families he was errand boy, soda jerk, grocery clerk and even factory hand before his twelfth birthday. He remembered his early life as 'lonely, nostalgic and uninspiring', typified by dingy hallways, drab houses and a monotony punctuated only by the ritual of a bath in a tin-tub every Saturday night. By the age of four or five he had

The New Grand Opera House, Evansville about 1910

begun to draw, and while other children played he would sit in the backyard drawing from flowers or copying reproductions of the dashing Wild West paintings of Frederic Remington.

His mother remarried, this time very happily, in 1899. Her second husband was John M. Rees, a miner. They lived together in Evansville for the next thirty years and Kauffer recalled that his step-father had encouraged his artistic aspirations. Kauffer left school at the age of 12 or 13 to be helper to the scene painter at Evansville's Grand Opera House. He was clearly precocious and by the age of 17 – unusually for a minor – he is listed as a painter in the City Directory.[4] The first listing, in 1907, probably coincides with Kauffer's departure from the town as scene-painter, barker and general help to a travelling repertory theatre. Looking back on his Evansville childhood late in life Kauffer said 'An environment like that has a propelling force to certain kinds of natures. You want to get out of it.'[5]

While he was with the travelling players he met the character actor Frank Bacon (1864–1922), who later became widely known as co-author and star of *Lightnin'*, a Broadway hit in 1918 and later a John Ford film. Bacon took to Kauffer and invited him to emigrate to California where he owned a fruit ranch. At least part of the time Kauffer seems to have worked on the ranch – probably in exchange for the time to paint. In 1910 Bacon left for the East Coast but first settled Kauffer in a position with the San Francisco bookseller and art dealer, Paul Elder. Kauffer's time on the ranch – perhaps a year – was later celebrated by an unusual portrait of him by the painter Maxwell Armfield. The picture, titled *The Californian*, shows Kauffer galloping naked over the plains on horse-back.[6]

Kauffer was taken on by Elder on condition that he would, within one month, 'learn the English language sufficiently to approach customers without his slangy stage jargon'.[7] In the Elder Bookshop and Art Rooms at 239 Grant Avenue Kauffer acquired not only a speaking voice of marked attractiveness and distinction but also a life-long passion for books. He continued his studies as a painter by receiving his first formal training at evening sessions at the Mark Hopkins Institute, a centre of the 'Californian Style' in easel and mural painting.[8]

A good customer of the bookshop was Joseph E. McKnight (1865–1942), Professor of Elementary Education at the University of Utah. The story of Kauffer's meeting Professor McKnight and the subsequent momentous result is told in a long letter Kauffer wrote to his parents on 1 August 1912. As it is the earliest surviving letter from Kauffer, and discloses something of his ardent and innocent nature, the letter is quoted here almost in full:

My dear Mother and Father
Can you believe it, that I'm going to Paris, France, to study. Its really and truly so. I'm so happy for it means that now at last the time has come and will be short for our being together for good – for just as soon as I return we shall make a home and a studio. Now I'll tell you how it all came about, *oh so* sudden. About two years ago a professor of the University of Utah came into the store, we became quite friends and corresponded, it seems as though at the very beginning he took a deep interest in me and my work. Of course nothing was said in particular, only that I had great talent. Last year during vacation he came in with his wife and daughter who is about ten years, and visited quite often, noting my progress, still time went on and I never gave Paris a thought. He returned again this year and visited a few times and saw my late advancement. Well yesterday he came in and said, 'I want to talk with you'.

Said he: 'Do you want to study?' 'You just bet I do', said I. Said he, 'Then you will, for I can help you'. Well – my goodness, what could I say – my life's dream come to life, and it seems like a fairy story. Its absolutely true and I will be home for a while to see you both, about October, if all goes well. Think of it dear ones, it doesn't seem possible does it? I know Mr McKnight well and that it is just his love of art to persuade a talented fellow along. Now of course this is a loan in a measure, that is, when I have made good I pay it back as I can, no hurry nor limited time, just when I'm successful – everyone is so certain that I am going to be a great painter that I know I will or else the way and means would not have opened up to me. He is a Christian Scientist, having overcome a great illness. Therefore I know his desire is purely that of humanity to progress – and a pure thought, for when I have paid it back it goes to some other struggling youth, who dreams of a great future, such as I have done. I know this is going to make you both happy, for it surely means that at last the sun is shining for us three. I attribute it to Science and my mother's great teaching to know the truth. God bless you mother dear, you have done it all, and He is going to let us three have the happiest days imaginable. I can't question your confidence in me, for I feel sure you know and feel that I will be successful, and the money borrowed will be a trifle compared to being successful. I figure on two years in Paris and that twelve hundred dollars or less will be the amount. I shall be economical, knowing full well that in that I'm helping another to gain his point. I shall study right along in my Science knowing that it will point the truth always and always. I don't want you to ever feel alarmed of the environment of Paris, for that is prevailing everywhere and a strong character knows the good from the bad. I am sure you don't question that, for I shall always stay the boy you wanted me to be, for I know the struggle that you, mother dear, went thru. I can see your face just beam with joy when you read the news, for it is the event of events, and the beauty of it is, it is just a loan, to be repaid whenever I can and when I have gained success.

Already the art critics from the *Call* and *Bulletin* have been in and received my story and also viewed what sketches I have and before I leave S.F. no doubt there will be quite a story, which all helps to make me known. Everyone is glad. Miss Taylor is away yet and does not know, but she will be too – I give my notice about the fifteenth of August – quit about September 20th. Stopover in Salt Lake City when Mr McKnight is to make the final arrangements then on to home to see you for a month and then the Red Star Line from Philadelphia for Paris, France, second class cabin. Write me soon and tell me how happy you are . . .

Ever your devoted and affect. son,
Ed[9]

A small exhibition of Kauffer's paintings was held at the Elder Art Rooms and Porter Garnett wrote an enthusiastic notice for the *San Francisco Call*.[10] In homage to his patron Kauffer adopted the name McKnight and was soon on his way to Europe. He stopped for a few months, however, in Chicago – and by chance saw one of the epoch-making exhibitions of the twentieth century.

Kauffer was a student at the Art Institute of Chicago from October 1912 to March 1913. He took classes in painting, anatomy, history of painting and lettering.[11] Perhaps he wished to improve his basic skills before he began the precious two years in Paris. He conserved his funds by 'stoking the lodging house boiler in the morning, clearing dishes in the student refectory at lunch and carrying a spear in the opera at night'.[12] At the end of the year he exhibited an oil painting, *The Inlet – California note*, and a chalk drawing, *Blackstone Hotel*, at the annual exhibition of the Art Students' League. The following March the great 'Armory Show' came to the Art Institute on tour from New York City. The 643 works in this exhibition introduced America at one blow to almost everything of major importance in European painting from Delacroix to Marcel Duchamp, whose *Nude Descending a Staircase* was only one of many masterpieces shown. America was already familiar with Impressionism, which was eagerly collected, but here were Cézanne, Gauguin, van Gogh, Matisse and other Fauves, the progress of Cubism up to 1912 represented by Picasso and Braque, Kandinsky and a group of German Expressionists, and recent sculptures by Brancusi and Duchamp-Villon.

Kauffer came upon the results of 40 years' experimentation in painting all at once, and in a tense and embattled atmosphere. No art exhibition in America had ever aroused such passions as the Armory Show. The press and public figures felt obliged to proclaim their opinions – and the prevailing general feeling was of sheer outrage. Even museum curators, teachers and students joined in the orgy of condemnation. One of the painters who had organized the exhibition wrote back to New York from Chicago: 'The students are a lot of rowdy roughnecks . . . All the instructors at the Institute are mad through, one even went so far as to take a big class of the students into the French Room and threw a virtual fit condemning Matisse.'[13] On the last night of the showing in Chicago members of the Art Students' League staged a mock trial and ritual stabbing of a dummy labelled Henri Hairmatress followed by the burning of travesties of Matisse's *Le Luxe* and *La Femme Bleue*. But by this time Kauffer had already left Chicago for Europe. He later spoke of his response to the exhibition as 'intuitive': 'I couldn't have spoken about it then. I didn't understand it. But I certainly couldn't dismiss it. I felt a kind of quickening.'[14] He took a boat from Baltimore which put in at Algiers and Naples, and he reached Venice by June 1913. He made for Paris by way of Munich, where he stayed for a month or two.[15]

At this period the Bavarian capital was a centre of experimental activity. Paul Klee noted in his diary some events of 1913 – an exhibition of Italian Futurism, a Nolde exhibition, Nijinsky and Karsavina dancing with the Ballet Russe, but 'the measure is still not full!! Even Schönberg is being performed, the mad melodrama *Pierrot Lunaire*! Burst, you philistine, methinks your hour is struck!'[16] How much of all this Kauffer witnessed is not known, but in Munich he came across something of specific importance for his later work. This was the poster art of Ludwig Hohlwein (1874–1949).

Hohlwein was the outstanding poster designer of the period between the Art Nouveau flourish of the 1890s and the rise of Functionalism after the First World War. A correspondent from the London art magazine *The Studio* wrote of the posters of Munich in 1912:

Posters summon you to the different beer-restaurants for concerts or carnival revels, announce some special brew, or the great drinking feasts of the Spring or the fairs of Autumn, the joyous Kermesse. These posters are, for the most part, characterised by sober elegance and fine harmony of tone, they do not 'shout' at you from the walls nor are they crude in colour – they attract by their undoubted good taste, and fix the attention of the passer-by with their excellent colouring.[17]

Hohlwein was himself a notable bon viveur and an aficionado of hunting and the turf. His first success was a poster advertising a fashionable Munich tailor, Hermann Scherrer. This shows a young man with riding crop, saddle, riding boots, and breeches in grey and white check – a bulldog at his feet. It is an image of international elegance based on English tailoring and fashion – Scherrer indeed chose to use the English words 'Breeches-Maker and Sporting Tailor' to describe himself. Chic of fashion is equalled by chic of advertising. A French correspondent for the Paris magazine *Art et Décoration* observed that copies of this poster were taken home by the young French and English dandies who visited the city.[18]

In posters, programme covers, trade-cards and other ephemera Hohlwein publicly defined a particular kind of elegance, and became 'well-known and deservedly appreciated, not only by an élite of artists and sportsmen, but by the general public' as the *Studio* writer observed. *Art et Décoration* went further, declaring that Hohlwein was conceivable without Munich, but not Munich without Hohlwein. At the time of the Armory Show Kauffer would have seen the quality that could be achieved in poster art, for the exhibition included Toulouse-Lautrec's *Le Divan Japonais*. Munich, however, would have provided his first opportunity of seeing the contribution a master poster artist could make to the surface of life in a cosmopolitan city.

Kauffer reached Paris in the autumn of 1913. Like other students he worked in the museums, in the afternoon sketch schools, and at the Académie Moderne – where his great French near-contemporary in poster art, A.M. Cassandre, was to begin his career some 10 years later. Given the immense amount of activity in all the arts in Paris at this date it would seem impossible to know what particularly impressed Kauffer. Fortunately a friend he made at that time, the Englishman Colin Hurry, was able to recall this.[19] Kauffer was interested in *everything*: 'Now he would be influenced by a friend, now by a book, now by the work of another painter, now by some aspect of nature.' More specifically, however, Hurry remembers that Kauffer talked of Matisse, Derain, Vlaminck and Chagall but that 'van Gogh was his hero-figure at this time'. In the spring of 1914 Kauffer went off to Normandy on a painting trip, taking with him van Gogh's *Letters*. A small oil painting of the Seine survives from this period and establishes Kauffer's discipleship to the milder aspects of van Gogh's style.[20]

On 7 July 1914 Kauffer married a gifted American concert pianist, Grace Ehrlich. She had been a pupil of Edward MacDowell in New York and was then studying under Isidore Philippe at the Paris Conservatoire. A close friend from the Paris period, Maria Zimmern Petrie, has described Grace Kauffer as 'highly intelligent, warm-hearted, a strong personality with a genius for teaching'.[21] Only a month after their marriage the young couple were obliged to leave Paris. War conditions made survival there impossible. By then Maria Zimmern Petrie had settled in Durham and they left for England to join her in August 1914.

Hohlwein's poster for Hermann Scherrer (about 1912)

E. McKnight Kauffer 1915 Painting by Maxwell Armfield

Chapter 2. **Painter into Designer**

'I DO NOT REMEMBER how he came to England', Sir Francis Meynell wrote after Kauffer's death, 'but when he came he was already the exquisite, the son of a hundred kings.'[1] Kauffer himself wrote that he felt at home for the first time. He liked the tranquillity of the landscape, the sense of roots and tradition.[2] In later notes he wrote he made it clear that he had come to England on his way to America – but 'liked the look of England and decided to stay'[3] His personality soon won him friends among painters and writers but his first years in Britain were hard. Maria Zimmern Petrie wrote:

We lived together for two or three months and Teddy tried hard to find a market for his beautiful textile designs or posters, tramping the streets of Newcastle for days. He painted and sketched at Durham, but a stop was put to that also, for the boys thought he was my brother and a spy [Maria Zimmern Petrie was German-born; her husband Eric had already enlisted on the English side] and boys began to throw stones at him. There seemed no possible chance for the couple to settle down anywhere in northern England and find a living, so we decided that they must try their luck in London.[4]

An oil painting by Kauffer of the Petries' house in Durham from this time shows that he was still under the spell of van Gogh.[5] In London the search for work was still hectic and living conditions difficult. Grace had of course no piano, so could neither play nor teach.

Teddy had to spend hours every night dishwashing to earn a living, and again tried every avenue to find a post as designer or artist or get commissions.[6]

Houses, Durham 1914

Kauffer had tried over 25 London companies unsuccessfully when he met John Hassall, one of the best-known poster artists of the day. Hassall advised him to try Frank Pick, the Publicity Manager of the London Underground Electric Railways.[7] Pick had been obliged, like every other publicity man, to cut back his programme because of war shortages of paper – but he gave Kauffer a commission. Kauffer's first posters appeared for the London Underground Railways in 1915. Over the next 25 years the company became his major client and he their major poster artist. The company gave Kauffer an audience of millions – in return he gave the company a succession of designs of sparkling originality and widespread influence. This important partnership owed much to Frank Pick – but also to the tradition of which Pick was a part. Tracing this is essential to the understanding not only of this one client but of the climate of opinion in which Kauffer worked in England.

FRANK PICK AND ADVERTISING

Frank Pick (1878–1941) came from non-conformist Lincolnshire stock and trained as a solicitor before joining the London and North Eastern Railways.[8] He rapidly became the golden boy of the company and when his chief, Sir George Gibb, became head of the Underground Electric Railways Co of London, Gibb shrewdly brought his assistant with him. They began work in 1906 and two years later Pick was put in charge of publicity. This was a department in which railway companies in general had a bad name. Speaking at a meeting on poster advertising in 1893 one commentator accused the London railway companies of spoiling the newly laid-out Embankment Gardens between Charing Cross and Temple Stations beside the Thames. The new vistas were closed by ugly painted boards which were useless as advertisements because 'no one sees them unless he sees the station, and those who go in quest of it certainly do not need this dirty kaleidoscope to embitter their approach'.[9]

More graphically, Rudyard Kipling likened the hoardings lining the London and South Western Railway to 'an Army and Navy Stores list in a nightmare'.[10] The speaker at the meeting in 1893 was Richardson Evans (1846–1928), one of the unsung heroes of advertising history, and the meeting resulted in the formation of SCAPA – the Society for Checking the Abuses of Public Advertising. This exemplary organization came into being to discipline the *laissez faire* outgrowth of advertising which occurred in all industrialized countries in the second half of the nineteenth century. In 1872 John Ruskin wrote from Florence:

the fresco-painting of the bill-sticker is likely, so far as I can see, to become the principal fine art of Modern Europe: here, at all events, it is now the principal source of street effect. Giotto's time is past, like Oderigi's; but the bill-poster succeeds. . . .[11]

Ruskin watched the priests of the Annunziata pasting up posters, with artfulness and ingenuity, between the statues of the great façade. In the Titianesque maiden who advertised Mrs Allen's Hair Restorer, 'with her flowing hair and equally flowing promises', he recognized the new madonna of the nineteenth century. In his years of retirement in the Lake District, boats with sails advertising Beecham's Pills were introduced to Lake Windermere. The Niagara Falls were littered over with giant-size advertisements in the 1870s. A little later William Dean Howells opened his novel *The Rise of Silas Lapham* (1885) with this inter-

Frank Pick 1915

Illustration from the *Graphic* 1893

view between the self-made Lapham and the bored journalist Bartley:

In less'n six months there wa'n't a board fence, nor a bridge girder, nor a dead wall, nor a barn, nor a face of rock in that whole region that didn't have 'Lapham's Mineral Paint – Specimen' on it in the three colours we began by making.

I've heard a good deal of talk about that S.T. – 1860 – X-man, and the stove-blacking man, and the kidney-cure man, because they advertised in that way; and I've read articles about it in the papers; but I don't see where the joke comes in, exactly. So long as the people that owns the barns and fences don't object, I don't see what the public has to do with it. And I never saw anything so very sacred about a big rock, along a river or in a pasture, that it wouldn't do to put mineral paint on it in three colours. . . . I say the landscape was made for man, and not man for the landscape.

Yes, said Bartley carelessly, it was made for the stove-polish man and the kidney-cure man.

In England the photographer Frank Meadow Sutcliffe, who was internationally admired in the 1880s and 90s for his pastoral landscape work, also trained his camera on advertising:

We have sometimes photographed ugliness for a lark, and have made lantern slides of bill-posting hoardings . . . of painted advertisements in beauty spots of somebody's pills, or someone's pianos, and have talked by the hour to big congregations, pointing out how much easier life would be if all such abominations were done away with, but all to no purpose.[12]

SCAPA, however, was very purposeful and very effective. It is familiar that in the 1890s many artists worked in the poster medium and that, in the hands of a Cheret, a Mucha or a Lautrec, posters became a great new medium of expression. It is a much less well-known fact that in the same years artists, architects and designers of equal distinction were deeply involved in posters from a quite different point of view. William Morris, Alfred Waterhouse, C.R. Ashbee, William Holman Hunt, Sir John Millais, Lord Leighton, Sir Edward Poynter, Walter Crane, George Bodley, Halsey Ricardo and C.F.A. Voysey – the backbone of the Royal Academy and the spearhead of the Arts and Crafts movement – were all members of SCAPA. Morris's last public appearance was made in support of SCAPA.[13] The Society's first Parliamentary success was the 1907 Advertisements Regulation Act which enabled local authorities to frame by-laws preventing disfigurement by advertisements in the specific categories 'beautiful landscape' and 'pleasure promenades and public parks'. In 1925 a second Act extended the principle to townscape in general, and the series of post-war Town and Country Planning Acts consolidated SCAPA's early achievement. Similar legislation was enacted in France in 1906, 1909 and 1912, while in America – where SCAPA's activities were watched with interest – this majestic Constitutional Amendment was passed in Massachusetts in 1918: 'Advertising in public ways, in public places, and on private property in public view may be regulated and restricted by law.'

SCAPA's President, the architect Alfred Waterhouse R.A., made two specific proposals for the improvement of advertising on London's Underground railways:

1. The spaces let for advertising to be clearly defined and to have some harmonious relation to the general [architectural] scheme.
2. The display on the main walls and the platform and fences to be confined to the more artistic forms of poster: and provision to be made for their frequent change.[14]

The London and North Eastern Railway had been more sensitive to SCAPA's proposals than any other line – even completely banning advertising in some country stations – and when Frank Pick took charge of publicity at the London Underground Electric Railways he did something quite simple. He put the Waterhouse proposals into effect. He disciplined the actual arrangement of the poster advertising within and without his stations, restricting them to partitioned areas, and, although he was not in a position to control the quality of advertising issued by other companies, he set about creating a standard for his own.

THE 'ARTISTIC' POSTER

It was decidedly an event when Fred Walker A.R.A. – the original of Little Billee in George du Maurier's *Trilby* – undertook the design of a poster for a stage production of Wilkie Collins's *The Woman in White* in 1871. The poster – 'as big as a door' – was printed from many engraved wood blocks fastened together. Lithography was at that moment taking over from wood engraving as the major production process for posters and in fact small lithographic copies of Walker's poster were also issued. Walker disliked the lithographic version but wrote to his wood engraver, Hooper: 'I am bent on doing all I can with a first attempt at what I consider might develop into a most important branch of the art.'

He had actually done no more before he died, prematurely, in 1875 but his example was remembered. In 1881 the *Magazine of Art* published Fred Walker's prophetic remarks for the first time in an article on 'The Streets as Art Galleries'. The magazine pointed out that the widely admired revival in the decorative arts and design had left the streets untouched:

Poster by Fred Walker 1871

> The art-student, the picture buyer, the patron of Mr Morris's wallpapers – these come from classes that already possess much cultivation, therefore much faculty for recreation and pleasant sentiment. But what about that great outside population – the artisan, the prisoner at the desk, the great multitude of men and women who exist drearily behind counters day after day, not forgetting sterner toilers still – do not all these need also to be trained, delighted, given an expanded faculty for pleasure?[15]

These noble words were drastically let down by what the magazine had to offer as an artistic poster. It published one specially designed by Hubert Herkomer, then A.R.A., later a full Royal Academician. The poster shows a 'sacra conversazione' on the steps of the temple of art – a design redolent of the banal uplift of the 'Palaces of Art' popular at the international exhibitions of the day. Although he minced his art, Herkomer did not mince his words, describing advertising as 'an insult hurled from every spare wall, scaffolding and conveyance' and urging serious artists to take control of the hoardings. Academicians contributed some staid designs to advertising, but a genuine poster craze developed in the 1890s. As Kauffer himself later wrote, the influence of Toulouse-Lautrec 'passed like a comet over the major part of the Western hemisphere'.[16] Edward Bella, the main promoter of the poster craze, claimed that 'in no other branch of design do the most characteristic features of everyday life find clearer and more drastic utterance than in the art of pictorial and mural advertising'.[17] An enthusiastic writer on 'The Collecting of Posters: A New Field for Connoisseurs' was led to travesty Ruskin's original remarks as 'Mr Ruskin's dictum that advertising is nowadays the only living art'.[18] A 'Poster Academy' was set up in London in 1901 with the aim of convincing advertisers that 'the artistic poster is more effective than an inartistic one'. John Hassall, Cecil Aldin, Dudley Hardy and James Pryde were on the committee, while one A.J. Munnings is mentioned in the membership.[19]

PICK'S EARLY POSTER CAMPAIGNS

Frank Pick regarded the entrances of his stations as shop windows in which the wares available from the service could be advertised. By making specific framed spaces for posters he could commission designs which would not have stood a chance on ordinary hoardings. His first commissions in 1908 set the tone for the next 30 years. There was a humorous poster by John Hassall, *No need to ask a p'liceman*, which drew attention to the new Underground railways map – which itself, under the hands of a series of designers, has become a classic of graphic design.[20] The printers Waterlows were responsible for producing the bulk of the company's letterpress notices and Pick went to an artist in their studio, Charles Sharland, for *The Valley of the Thames*. Sharland was not an assured landscape artist but he came up with imaginative solutions for some of Pick's more out of the way schemes. In 1912 he designed a poster occasioned by an eclipse of the sun, explaining which stations were closest to London's seven hills for the benefit of eclipse-watchers. Fred Taylor, a commercial artist just beginning to emerge as a free-lance, contributed *Hampstead Fair*.

News of improved services, news of events, and reminders of the open spaces within easy reach of central London – these were the typical themes of Pick's poster campaigns. A more romantic note was struck in 1910 when Pick commissioned two posters on the theme 'The Moving Spirit of London'. Alfred France produced an image of Botticellian nymphs gliding beneath the city. T.R. Way – formerly assistant to and biographer of Whistler – was more up to date with an image of the Lots Road Power Station in twilight, but the caption seems to be Pick's own characteristic contribution:

> This Power House burns 500 tons of coal a day
> It contains 8 Turbo Generators
> Running at 1000 r.p.m.
> Developing 65,000 Horse-Power
> To work 80 miles of railway
> 145 lifts and 900 cars
> For the use and benefit of the People of London.[21]

Although the Arts and Crafts Exhibition Society had many members who supported SCAPA's aims, none had contributed to the improvement of poster design. In 1912 Pick commissioned the heraldry artist Macdonald Gill for his famous *Wonderground* map – and in 1916 the Society included lithographic posters (for the Underground) in its exhibition for the first time. The most significant and fruitful link between Pick and the Arts and Crafts movement came in 1913 when he commissioned a new alphabet for the company from the greatest calligrapher of modern times, Edward Johnston. Johnston Sans Serif made its appearance in 1916. Its effect has been described by Noel Rooke:

It was a breathtaking surprise to nearly all who could be interested. The very lowest category of letter had been suddenly lifted to a place among the highest. We can scarcely now understand how revolutionary a proceeding it seemed. In this definite 'Utility' letter he had used subtleties till then only found in the best of the Roman inscriptions.[22]

At the same time Johnston provided the Underground with its familiar symbol, which remains among the most serenely successful logotypes in existence. Such imaginative commissions go a long way towards justifying the evaluation of Pick's career made after his death by Christian Barman:

Not since Wedgwood has an English tradesman done so much to make his trade a spiritual asset to the society on which it feeds. His chief merit was this, that he showed us a new type of business executive, cultured, sensitive, and creative in the highest sense, which modern business will have to produce if our material civilization is to keep what little of humanity still clings to it.[23]

Not least, Frank Pick's example provided a pattern which other businesses followed, and this made possible Kauffer's brilliantly successful work in British advertising over the 25 years from 1915 to 1940.

KAUFFER'S FIRST POSTERS

Looking back at Pick's work much later, Kauffer discounted the philanthropic intention – he argued that Pick was creating goodwill for the company by respecting the public and that he was 'selling traffic'.[24] Kauffer's first four posters are essentially gouache or poster paint landscapes, indicating open spaces relatively distant from central London but served either by the company's trains or buses. *Oxhey Woods* (plate 2), *In Watford* (plate 1), *Reigate: Route 60* and *North Downs* (the last two dated 1915 but issued in 1916) offer a fascinating view of Kauffer's stylistic impressionableness at the outset of his poster career. The boldly painted outlines of *Oxhey Woods*, which is probably the earliest of the four, can be attributed to Kauffer's continuing interest in van Gogh – black lines describing a yellow path, blue lines for the outlines of a brown tree. The van Gogh notes are augmented, however, by touches from a milder tradition seen in the system of gentle, late Art Nouveau curves which runs through the scheme, and the child-like treatment of trees and toadstools. This almost recalls the children's books of Mabel Lucie Attwell, but these features and the lettering are probably due to contact with Maxwell Armfield, who painted two portraits of Kauffer in 1915, and suggest influence from the Birmingham Group.[25] *In Watford* is a purer manifestation of van Gogh in design, drawing conventions and a colour treatment, notably in the blue trees, which is well on the way to becoming Fauve. The wooden foot-bridge over the lake at Watford strongly recalls similar constructions in Japanese pleasure gardens and suggests that Kauffer had returned to one of van Gogh's sources of inspiration – Japanese colour woodcuts. This supposition is borne out by a change in Kauffer's style of signature. *In Watford* and *Oxhey Woods* are signed in a way which loosely recalls Ludwig Hohlwein's style of signature. The 'E. McKnight' is on one line, 'Kauffer' below it on a second line, the two joined by a diagonal flourish. In *Reigate: Route 60*, in which the tree trunks are pure scarlet, and fields yellow and red, Kauffer has arrived at poster-Fauvism – but now the signature is an orientalizing 'E.K.' enclosed in a box, much in the manner of a Japanese woodcut master's monogram. Kauffer recognized Japanese prints as the inspiration of Toulouse-Lautrec's innovations in poster design – 'his admiration for the Japanese print amounted almost to worship'.[26]

This classic source reappears, breathtakingly transformed, in at least two of Kauffer's finest designs, although in both cases the original models are masked by Kauffer's interest in a new and local style – English Vorticism. Nothing could be further from the 'Earthly Paradise' idylls of the Birmingham Group which seem to touch Kauffer's *Oxhey Woods* than Vorticism. The temper of Vorticism could be summarized as urban, abstract and short – defining itself at the premises of the Rebel Art Centre, in two issues of the magazine *Blast*, in polemics by Wyndham Lewis and Ezra Pound – whose Imagist aesthetics are the closely related by-product in poetry – and at a controversial group exhibition held at the Doré Gallery in London in 1915. In the catalogue introduction Wyndham Lewis wrote of Vorticism as an antidote to 'an immense commercialised mass of painting and every other form of art . . . a load of sugary, cheap, anecdotal and in every way pitiable muck poured out by the ton'.

It seems likely that Kauffer saw this exhibition and even more certain that he read Lewis's remarks on how Vorticism would impinge directly on the public:

Let us give a direct example of how this revolution will work in popular ways. In poster advertisement by far the most important point is a telling design. Were the walls of London carpeted with abstractions rather than the present mass of work that falls between two stools, the design usually weakened to explain some point, the effect architecturally would be much better, and the Public taste could thus be educated in a popular way to appreciate the essentials of design better than picture galleries have ever done.

The history of the mutual interaction of advertising design and modern art has yet to be written, but behind Lewis's remarks we can range Marinetti's celebration of posters in a Futurist manifesto in Italy, and an apposite comment by Apollinaire on the painter Fernand Léger in Paris. Much as Vorticism denounced Futurism as mere 'impressionism of speed' the movement was fuelled by Futurist aesthetics. In *War, the world's only hygiene* (1911–15) Marinetti urged poets and painters to celebrate 'Multicoloured billboards on the green of the fields, iron bridges that chain the hills together, surgical trains that pierce the blue belly of the mountains, enormous turbine pipes, new muscles of the earth'.[27] In a lecture attended by Apollinaire in 1914, Léger defined a new urban realism in painting. 'Himself a peasant', Apollinaire reflected, 'he knew that peasants who are not shocked to see a poster in their fields have not succumbed to bad taste but have simply learned to savour a necessary reality'.[28] Curiously enough Wyndham Lewis's words seem to be a direct prediction of Kauffer's first major work, *Flight*, which was designed in 1916. This image is also the finest invention of his entire career, became his talisman in the later years of disillusion, and may even provide the key to understanding his personality.

FLIGHT 1916

Kauffer and his wife stayed in the little village of Blewbury, near Didcot in Berkshire, in the summer of 1916. Blewbury remains as picturesque as its name and has long been an artist's colony. As well as thatched cottages there is a group of wooden summer studios. The Kauffers took the Policeman's Cottage and neighbours during their stay included Alvin Langdon Coburn, the American photographer, Kenneth Grahame and his wife – the setting seems ideal for the author of *The Wind in the Willows* – and Miss S.B. Webster, who (as Susan Beatrice Pearse) illustrated the 'Ameliaranne' books. She wrote of Kauffer over 50 years later:

I knew him fairly well at that time and admired his intense devotion to Art – he saw beauty in everything and his aim was to get to the core of that beauty to share with others. He would follow the flight of birds until he had got the rhythm and harmony of motion which he would interpret in his own way. No detail escaped him. He had a child-like wonder and admiration for nature.[29]

Kauffer's only statement about *Flight* was made in 1950:

The design *Flight* was not invented in a studio. It came after much observation of birds in flight. The problem seemed to me at any rate a translation into design terms of three factors, namely, bird identification, movement, and formalization into pattern and line. Birds in flight and aeroplane formations are singularly alike. The arrowhead thrust is the dominant motif. But wings have a contrary movement – so this too has to be considered. . . .[30]

The design is also Kauffer's homage to Vorticism. Woodcuts were a primary vehicle for several Vorticist artists, notably Edward Wadsworth and David Bomberg, and were familiar from the pages of *Blast*. A woodcut by Kauffer of *Flight* is probably the earliest surviving stage in its design.[31] The second known version was published in an interesting context in January 1917. It appeared in the magazine *Colour* which reserved a page in each monthly issue as a 'Poster Gallery'. Artists were invited to submit designs for free publication on this page and advertisers were invited to buy them for publicity use. Comparison between the woodcut and the version in *Colour* shows how skilfully Kauffer refined his idea. The wings in the woodcut are serrated – these are straightened out in the second version, which enhances the

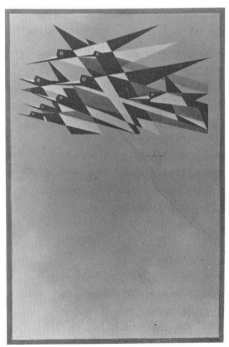

impression of speed. The legibility of the design was improved by dividing the light and dark areas less geometrically but more aptly, the number of birds was reduced from eight to seven, and they were – suitably – given a great deal of 'air'. The second version was improved again in a final version, dated 1918. The version shown in *Colour* had the disadvantage of making the group of birds into a solid mass which tends to 'drop' through the space below. In the 1918 version the pattern of birds is linked to the borders of the poster. This small alteration emphasizes flat, surface quality and stresses the idea of rapid onward transition (plate 4).

Flight 1916 (2nd version)

Flight 1916 Woodcut

The subject matter was new to Vorticism but not to Futurism. Giacomo Balla painted a series of pictures based on his observation of the flight of swifts in Rome in the late summer and autumn of 1913, and an example from the series was published in Boccioni's *Pittura e Scultura Futurista* in 1914. A comparison of Balla's interpretation with Kauffer's shows the essential difference in aims between Futurism and Vorticism as clearly as it shows the underlying similarities. Balla's work could be regarded as 'impressionism of speed', rendered in large wave-like rhythms. His observations were reinforced by study of E.J. Marey's photographic analysis of bird flight. Kauffer's observations were reinforced from a very different source. Once again he used a Japanese model. It seems likely that a flight of small birds, printed predominantly in green, yellow and grey in an illustrated sketchbook of birds, flowers, insects and fishes published in Japan in 1820, was his model. Kauffer used black and khaki but retained the optimistic flavour of his model by using bright yellow as the ground.[32]

Suiseki, *Flight of birds* 1820

Extraordinarily enough, this revolutionary design actually was used in a poster campaign. Kauffer later said that it was sold – presumably after being seen in *Colour* magazine – to an advertising agent and that he was paid 50 dollars.[33] It seems likely that the agent was T.B. Lawrence, who later commissioned designs from Kauffer. However, it was re-sold to Francis Meynell. Meynell, later Sir Francis, organized a brilliant poster campaign for the Labour newspaper the *Daily Herald* when it was launched on 31 March 1919.[34] The paper's editor, George Lansbury, promised in the first issue to 'voice the aspirations of Labour. We shall work unceasingly for a revolution, peaceful but complete, which shall destroy the present system of competition and force and replace it by the rule of cooperation'. Meynell recognized Kauffer's image, which he captioned 'Soaring to Success, the Early Bird', as 'a flight of birds that might almost be a flight of aeroplanes; a symbol, in those days of hope, of the unity of useful invention and natural things'.[35] A similar metaphor appears in the pages of Laszlo Moholy-Nagy's book *Malerie, Fotografie, Film* published in the optimistic days of the Bauhaus in the mid-1920s: on one page he illustrated a flock of cranes in flight, 'A fine organization of light and shade in itself', and opposite it he showed a flight of seaplanes over the Arctic – 'Repetition as a space-time motif'.

Night Rays (about 1920)
Painting by Frank Medworth
showing Early Bird poster on hoarding

Kauffer's design exactly expressed the aspirations of the radical newspaper and the more general hopes of the post-war period of 'Reconstruction'. A strikingly similar image occurs in a famous poem by

Siegfried Sassoon, first literary editor of the *Daily Herald*. The poem, 'Everyone Sang', was written when Sassoon heard that the Armistice had been signed:

Everyone suddenly burst out singing;
And I was filled with such delight
As prisoned birds must find in freedom
Winging wildly across the white
Orchards and dark green fields; on; on; and out of sight.

Everyone's voice was suddenly lifted,
And beauty came like the setting sun.
My heart was shaken with tears and horror
Drifted away. . . . O but every one
Was a bird; and the song was wordless; the singing will never be done.[36]

Sassoon later added, in *Siegfried's Journey: 1916–20*, that 'the singing that would never be done was the Social Revolution which I believed to be at hand'. Kauffer's friend Colin Hurry wrote of him in 1921 that 'He belongs to no political party, unless a fierce pity for the underdog makes him a Socialist. He wants to see equality of opportunity established for everyone else, though he has never asked for it himself.'[37]

As a model of poster design *Flight* even came to the attention of Winston Churchill, who sent for Kauffer with a view to commissioning a flag for the Royal Air Force. Apparently Churchill's enthusiasm waned on discovering that the artist was an American citizen, and when Kauffer declined to adopt British citizenship at his request the matter was dropped.[38] Many years later, however, one of Kauffer's English disciples, Theyre Lee-Elliott, provided a flying bird symbol for Imperial Airways (to be seen on a Kauffer poster in the plates). Lee-Elliott's symbol (1934) continued in use with British Overseas Airways Corporation and a variant design of it now graces the British Airways/Air France Concord. *Flight* may seem ahead of its time but it fulfils very accurately the idea of the perfect poster as expressed by James Joyce's Leopold Bloom. Towards the close of *Ulysses*, first published in 1922, the advertising salesman Bloom meditates (nocturnally):

Upon some one sole unique advertisement to cause passers to stop in wonder, a poster novelty, with all extraneous accretions excluded, reduced to its simplest and most efficient terms not exceeding the span of casual vision and congruous with the velocity of modern life.[39]

DESIGNS AND PAINTINGS 1916–21

Kauffer later wrote that 'when I began advertising design in England in 1916, the outstanding work then was of the Munich realistic school, more pictorial than poster. My enthusiasm, to counteract that influence, was at first by violent methods, but such designs as I did were confined to exhibition posters for the then modern group of painters known as the London Group, of which I was secretary.'[40] During the five-year period 1916–21 Kauffer was an increasingly exhibited painter who seemed to be at home with all of the different, and sometimes warring, elements of the English avant-garde, but he was also an increasingly successful designer. His remarks above are a little misleading. The *Flight* design was not immediately followed by consistent Vorticist experimentation in poster design. Instead Kauffer actually adopted the style of Munich school realism. Further contributions to the Poster Gallery page in *Colour* can be exactly paralleled in Hohlwein. In the issue of February 1917, for example, Kauffer offered a

Bale labels 1921

favourite Hohlwein idea – a flunkey in period costume offering a box which might contain expensive chocolates or cigars. A month later Kauffer contributed a design of a boy on a donkey. This again fits comfortably into the prevailing Munich style – but this time the poster was bought and duly appeared for the Kensington department store Derry and Toms as *Economy and Smartness in Men's Wear*, together with a boating scene issued as *Now Proceeding – Summer Sale at Derry and Toms*.

A more interesting commission for which Kauffer produced designs throughout this period was initiated by the Manchester textile company Steinthal & Co. A.P. Simon, head of the firm, was an early buyer of Vorticist paintings and subsequently active in the Design and Industries Association. His partner William Zimmern – a cousin of the Kauffers' friend Maria Zimmern Petrie – commissioned Kauffer in 1916 to design a set of bale labels for use on cotton goods exported by Steinthals to South America. These were colour lithographs of 5 × 3 inches which were intended to make identification of the bales easy at a glance. Kauffer's designs were at the outset in his typical early style, but he proved that even ephemeral trade labels could be treated resourcefully and memorably. The series eventually closed, at a total of 36, in 1928.[41] Further landscape posters were commissioned by Pick in 1916, plus a set of season ticket advertisements for which Kauffer made a series of humorous line drawings. Already he was moving away from the traditional area of the 'art poster' into what is more properly graphic design.

Until 1921 Kauffer regarded himself as a painter. Early English painter friends included the post-Impressionists Robert Bevan and his wife Stanislawa de Karlowska, whose Sunday 'At Homes' in Hampstead the Kauffers frequented. Through the Bevans Kauffer came to know other painters of similar temperament and talent, including Charles Ginner and Harold Gilman. They were all members of the London Group, which had replaced the New English Art Club as the effective meeting-point for new painting and sculpture. Kauffer exhibited with the London Group from June 1916 – when Epstein's *Rock Drill* (which fused a robot-like man, complete with an actual pneumatic drill, with motifs suggestive of a vulture's hooked head) was the principal new work shown. A month earlier Kauffer had his first one-man exhibition in England. This was held at Hampshire House in Hammersmith. The pictorialist photographer M.O. Dell was Secretary and the introduction to Kauffer's catalogue was written by the American Alvin Langdon Coburn, who was the first and only Vorticist photographer. Coburn's distinguished early work included his book of portraits *Men of Mark* and he made a portrait of Grace Kauffer for a projected volume – which was never published – of *Women of Note*. Coburn and Kauffer both made pictures from Coburn's studio looking over the Thames beside Hammersmith Bridge.[42] Kauffer's exhibition included still-life paintings and landscapes from Normandy, Kent, Brighton, Berkshire and London. He also exhibited six of his Underground posters. Coburn described the work as 'realistic without ever becoming commonplace, brilliant in colour but never harsh' and valued the paintings for their 'cheerfulness, their intense optimism'.[43]

In the autumn of 1916 Kauffer became a member of the London Group, and he and Grace took on the burden of its administration in the following spring when he became Secretary. He also joined the 'Cumberland Market Group' which included Paul Nash, a talented painter who worked – like Kauffer – in a number of design fields in the next two decades. As Secretary of the London Group Kauffer designed exhibition posters and abstract symbols for catalogue covers. These reflect Vorticist style and take Kauffer beyond his dependence on the Munich school. He was still, however, principally a painter and in 1917 the most influential critic of the day, Roger Fry, provided the introduction to an exhibition Kauffer held at the Birmingham Repertory Theatre. Fry wrote:

> He is one of the younger artists working in this country, whose aims may be taken as characteristic of the present phase of the new movement. His earlier work followed closely on the general lines of Cézanne's methods – more recently the influence of Cubism has been apparent, but has scarcely amounted to more than an increasing definition and delimitation of planes, and a slightly more abstract planning of the design. He has not allowed it to interfere with his direct sensibility to the forms and colours of natural objects. He seems to me to be exploring the possibilities in this direction with a view to discovering his own personal equation – the just balance between his acute and delicate sensibility, and his desire for logical precision and completeness of statement.[44]

Fry's support for Kauffer was generous. He kept a portfolio of Kauffer's drawings on sale at his Omega Workshops – a venture which encouraged painters to decorate furniture, pottery, toys and clothes and design mural schemes and carpets – and he included Kauffer's Birmingham exhibition in a larger show he organized at Heal's Gallery in the autumn of 1917, *New Movements in Art*. Fry was incorrect about the Cézanne influence, which only occurs in 1917 after Kauffer's van

Grace Kauffer (about 1916)
Photograph by Alvin Langdon Coburn

Sunflowers 1917 Oil painting

Trees 1918 Water-colour

Gogh period. However, Fry's summing up is a good general description and apt in regard to what was perhaps Kauffer's major painting – a large oil, *Sunflowers* (1917). That Kauffer set special store by this painting is suggested by the price he put on it in the London Group catalogue for the autumn exhibition in 1917: £50 instead of his usual £20 or less (although it is larger than any other surviving painting). He also made a woodcut version of the composition.

The Kauffers joined Maria Zimmern Petrie in a house she had taken at Edinburgh in 1918. A long letter from Fry shows the kind of painter Kauffer hoped to be:

My dear Kauffer

I was glad to get yr. letter and very much interested in yr. reflections on art. The whole question of groups and competition is very difficult. Art generally seems to flourish only when there are enough people interested in the same kind of thing to create a kind of spiritual high tension: the inspiration seems to come in waves and flourish in groups and yet perhaps the greatest work is done by the solitaries who withdraw like Cézanne when once they have caught the general idea and who work it out in independence. Anyhow the kind of competition of most of our groups, competition in the sense to épater, is worse than useless, and I daresay you will get there quicker for being away from it. Though frankly I shall miss yr. criticism and help. There are so few people in London who care at all seriously or intelligently that I looked on you as a great accession of strength to the little circle of enthusiasts that I am always dreaming [?] of keeping together in London. All the same I think it might really be more necessary for you than for most to work out yr. salvation alone. If I am right I expect you are one of those who will take a long time to discover yr. own artistic personality – I speak feelingly for I doubt if I am more than just beginning to do so at my horrible age. There are some personalities so tight and compact that they stick out at once and never change – often enough they are very small ones and incapable of growth and these do their best work at once, at 30 they have nothing more to discover and can only exploit. But there are others who have a great deal of taste and sensibility and intellect all of which tend to obscure the individual core but make it all the more richer when once the harmony of all these qualities comes to light and I suspect that you are one of that kind, which will mean a slow and laborious development with many doubts and misgivings. But I feel sure you have the character to face all that – it's as often as not lack of some sort of decent morale that ruins our artists here in London and makes them cynically accept a cheap success.[45]

Fry's assessment is borne out by Lord Clark, who remarked that 'Kauffer's personal distinction and integrity cannot be overrated'.[46] The stay in Edinburgh saved the Kauffers' funds – they were desperately poor – but soon they were on the way back to London, as Kauffer was at last accepted as a volunteer in the American army. On the train from Edinburgh to London they heard the news that the First World War had ended.[47]

THE ARTS LEAGUE OF SERVICE 1919

Very typical of the immediate period of post-war optimism was the foundation of the Arts League of Service in the spring of 1919. The ALS was founded after a big meeting at the studio of the dancer Margaret Morris: 'Energies set free after four years of destruction were seeking a new, peaceable, and above all constructive outlet. The possibilities of the opening of new fields of work were enormous'.[48] The first initiative was a lecture series on 'Modern Tendencies in Art' – Wyndham Lewis on painting, T.S. Eliot on poetry, Eugene Goossens on music, Margaret Morris on dancing. Kauffer was from the first a member of the Artists' subcommittee and wrote on poster design in the opening issue of the *ALS Bulletin*:

Few people realise the importance of the hoardings. It is from them that the masses gather ideas for a great many things that directly influence them. Now that England, after a pause of a dozen years, is again interested in the poster, let this feeling be so genuine and broadcast as to make the hoardings amusingly interesting and vitally important.

Kauffer designed the ALS symbol and took part in an exhibition of *Practical Arts* held at the Twenty-one Gallery in the winter of 1919. He contributed designs for a poster and a cretonne, (his first textile design), but more ambitiously a scheme for a 'Model Public House'. Edward Wadsworth sent in a Vorticist 'suggestion for a Building'. This provocative fortress of points and angles was illustrated, with Kauffer's pub, on the front page of the *Daily Mirror* on 18 November 1919. The Kauffer pub is a severe and centralized building, furnished with chairs reminiscent of C.R. Mackintosh, and decorated with murals. The nude figures in these derive from the typical Omega Workshops productions of Roger Fry, Duncan Grant and Vanessa Bell.

A travelling repertory theatre was one of the best-known ALS programmes during the early 1920s and Kauffer regularly provided posters and also sets and costumes. The ALS's call for artists to exercise their gifts 'for the things of everyday life' was also taken up by the 'Friday Club' which arranged an applied art display including Bernard Leach pottery, painted tiles by Macdonald Gill, silk designs by Mackintosh, label and poster designs by Albert Rutherston, textile designs by Paul Nash and – by this time inevitably – a group of posters by Kauffer.[49] Kauffer's leadership in the field was established by the *Daily Herald*'s use of *Flight*. Post-war possibilities encouraged Derry and Toms to take a more adventurous Kauffer design than the earlier ones – a *Winter Sales* poster in 1919 which is the first on a theme which drew the best from Kauffer in a subsequent series for the Underground. Vorticism surfaced again in a poster for Vigil Silks in the same year – Kauffer's design successfully adapts the style to the patterns of plain stripes typical of the firm's productions. Other Vorticist-derived symbols by Kauffer were used for the important quarterly *Art and Letters* and on the poster of the last London Group exhibition in which he showed – in spring 1919.

X GROUP 1920

Kauffer contacted former Vorticists such as Wyndham Lewis in July 1919, presumably hoping to take up the promise made in the 1915 issue of *Blast*: 'We shall not stop talking about culture when the war is over.' Lewis himself was keen to do some more 'Blasting': 'The present London Group is a bad working collection of individuals and will not improve.'[50] What Kauffer had in mind is clear from a letter Lewis wrote to the New York collector John Quinn: as well as exhibiting together, the group were to take 'a shop or office, where it is proposed to sell objects made by them, paintings and drawings, to a certain extent, and especially to have a business address from which the poster, cinematograph and other industries can be approached'. The business touch is surely Kauffer's, an attempt to advance the synthesis achieved in *Flight* – uniting experimental painting and experimental design.

With Lewis's energy pushing it along a group was formed, a gallery found, the name X Group adopted. The members – of whom there were 10 (a possible explanation for the X) – resigned en bloc from the London

A.L.S. symbol 1922

X Group poster 1920

Self Portrait 1920
Pen, ink and wash drawing

Utamaro, *Ladies caught in rain squall* 1801

Oil refinery 1921 Oil on metal

Group and a minor sensation occurred in spring 1920. Each artist contributed a woodcut self-portrait to the catalogue and these were all reproduced in the *Graphic* for 17 April. 'X' was hardly a unifying symbol and Lewis's evasive introduction to the catalogue did not suggest any real future for the group. The exhibition itself was the last flourish of Vorticism. Lewis's interest in the project seems mainly to have been the opportunity to affront Roger Fry, then influential in the London Group. The resignations were one thing, getting X Group's show into the Mansard Gallery ahead of the London Group was another minor triumph for Lewis. Kauffer's friend Colin Hurry lamely identified, in an article of 1921, the mysterious 'X' as 'the unknown which all artists should be seeking'. Kauffer's client at Vigil Silk, Alec Walker, took the show to Yorkshire and there the matter ended.

For Kauffer himself the exercise revived the memory of his brilliant earlier fusion of Vorticism and Japanese colour woodcuts. Among his finest designs is the Underground poster *Winter Sales* of 1921 (plate 6). Roger Fry later wrote of this particular design when he described 'the alacrity and intelligence people can show in front of a poster which if it had been a picture in a gallery would have been roundly declared unintelligible. The judicious frame of mind evidently slows the wits very perceptibly.' Fry wrote of Kauffer's design – a highly abstracted scene of elegant figures in a rainy London street – as a 'fascinating silhouette of dark forms to begin with, and out of these forms gradually disengage themselves hints of the flutter of mackintoshes blown by a gusty wind, of the straining forms pushing diagonally against the driving rain. In fact, all the familiar shapes of such a scene are taken as the bricks to build up a most intriguing pattern. But they demand a rather quick-witted recognition of slight indications for the design to become intelligible.'

The flat diagonal stripes which represent rain are taken direct from Japanese colour print conventions but so too is a great deal of the composition. A remarkably similar group of figures caught in a squall of rain, their umbrellas forming abstract patterns, was published by Utamaro in 1801. It seems likely that Kauffer once more fused Vorticism and a Japanese source. Writing of Toulouse-Lautrec's similar use of this source, Kauffer said that Lautrec 'did not imitate. He emulated its simplicity, finding Western types in the Music Halls and Cafés, that, eccentric as they were, could be adapted to the Japanese atmosphere of his compositions.'[51] So Kauffer's design is, in fact, a three-way synthesis: Utamaro, Lautrec, Lewis. As such it is, paradoxically, pure Kauffer.

While X Group collapsed Kauffer found greater success as a poster designer. Pick followed up his earlier commissions by asking in 1920 for 14 landscape posters, with more to follow in 1921. Kauffer's career as a painter finished in 1920 with his resignation from the London Group, the failure of X Group – and, perhaps, with the birth of his daughter Ann in October. Kauffer now found a hypocrisy in maintaining distinctions between 'pure' and commissioned work.[52] After the attempt to unite them in X Group had failed, Kauffer abandoned easel painting. There was one technical exception. In 1921 Kauffer provided a set of oil paintings illustrating oil refining processes and the originals were displayed on hoardings outside the Shell company headquarters in London while a new building was being constructed at 'Shell Corner' (Kingsway and Aldwych). Thereafter, as Lewis later put it, Kauffer 'disappeared as it were belowground, and the tunnels of the "Tube" became thenceforth his subterranean picture galleries'.[53]

E. *McKnight Kauffer* 1922 Photograph by Neal Walden

Chapter 3. **The Early Twenties**

IN 1921 Kauffer was sufficiently in funds to attempt to establish himself as a designer in New York. On a visit to London in 1920 Robert Allerton Parker, director of the Arts and Decoration Gallery in New York, had sought out Kauffer. An exhibition of 100 works was subsequently arranged and shown at Parker's gallery at 48–50 West 47th Street from 17–30 October 1921. Leaving his wife and daughter in London, Kauffer went over for the show and stayed for several months trying to find commissions. Parker also ran *Arts and Decoration* magazine and he wrote up Kauffer in the November issue, drawing attention to something that was already of importance for Kauffer: 'He claims that personal contact with the men requiring advertising art in the exploitation of their products is an absolute necessity in obtaining good results.' The article was titled 'E. McKnight Kauffer: A Commercial Artist with Ideals'. Kauffer contributed an article to the same issue. He moved straight on to the attack, his targets being know-nothing designers and complacent publicity men. He charged that ordinary designers presume to be specialists without ever having investigated the properties of their medium: 'Non-representative and geometrical pattern designs can in effect strike a sledge hammer blow if handled by a sensitive designer possessing a knowledge of the action of colour on the average man or woman. Knowledge of a similar nature is involved in the uses made of masses and line movements.'

This quasi-scientific point of view occurs on a number of occasions in Kauffer's writings in the early 1920s. There are good reasons for thinking that he was close at this period to the English Vorticist Edward Wadsworth. The source of Kauffer's analytical interest in colour and form may well derive from Wadsworth's translations, published in *Blast*, from Kandinsky's book *On the Spiritual in Art* – a title which would at once have aroused Kauffer's interest. It is also likely that Kauffer was well aware of the gift for formal analysis of his friend Roger Fry, whose approach was most widely disseminated in *Vision and Design* published in 1920. 'The Poster', Kauffer insisted in his article, 'has an interpretive vision, and is not imitative slavery . . . an intense realism may be more real than a photograph because of its power of suggestion.' And 'Posters are telegrams'. The last remark can be compared with A.M. Cassandre's formulation that a poster is a 'machine à annoncer'.[1]

Kauffer was struck by a contradiction between the pace of life in New York City, with its dynamic neon lighting, and the static prettiness of its posters. The business of advertising was to match actual urban pace, so that a poster could become an incident on the street as real as seeing a fire-engine at speed:

The fascination the public has for the race of fire apparatus is mainly colour and movement – the romance of fire is further back of the head. The swift flash of red, the glitter of the engine, the slender arrow of a hook and ladder, make the public feel differently for a few moments, long enough to have fixed a definite impression upon the mind.

Kauffer showed exactly what he meant in a poster designed directly he returned to England (see below). His exhibition received a friendly notice in the *New York Times* for 16 October 1921 and Kauffer was given a hero's welcome when he visited Evansville to see his parents the following February. A banquet in his honour was held in the Pompeiian Room of the Hotel McCurdy. A local paper records the occasion with some pride, detailing table decorations in pink, a basket of Columbia roses as a centrepiece and smaller baskets of winter lilacs and calendula at each end of the table. This was not all: 'Pink candles in crystal holders illuminated the table. The place cards were miniature palettes with brush and the favors were Columbia roses.' Kauffer's doings were regularly reported to readers of the *Evansville Courier* and *Evansville Journal*.[2] An exhibition was arranged in the studio of a professional photographer in the town, Neal Walden, and Walden's photograph of Kauffer taken on this visit is one of the earliest surviving photographs of him.

A press-cutting also records that Kauffer befriended a young painter called 'Birchfield', described as working in a factory in the Mid-West, and that Kauffer attempted to promote the artist on his return to London. This may well have been Charles Burchfield, who exhibited successfully at the Grosvenor Gallery in London in 1923 and became one of America's better-known painters in the 1930s. Either way, the story is typical of Kauffer's generosity towards other artists, which many of his friends have stressed. Kauffer's visit to the United States was not, however, a success. Already in England his position was supported by a few innovators in publicity – but in the United States his work fell on less well-prepared ground. He did a small commission for the Manhattan Electrical Supply Co – a pack for radio headsets. And he did find one important client – Theatre Guild in New York. He designed large-scale posters for Theatre Guild's 1922 productions of Bernard Shaw's *Back to Methuselah* and Leonid Andreyev's *He Who Gets Slapped*. These must have been very large as they were described as too big to be shown in Kauffer's next major exhibition of posters, held in 1925. Their size may account for the fact that no surviving copies of them are known. The *Evansville Courier* described them as 'mammoth', which was probably correct (even though the possibility of confusion arises as the poster for *Back to Methuselah* is dominated by a mammoth!). Kauffer may have got the commission, a valuable one, too late in his stay to affect the outcome of his visit. He later said that, despite his favourable press, he 'did not go down' and 'experienced a great rebuff'.[3] He returned to London in the spring of 1922.

KAUFFER IN LONDON: EARLY 1920s

Practically unknown in New York, Kauffer was by contrast almost a national figure in England by the early 1920s. His place in English cultural life is made beautifully clear in a passage from Evelyn Waugh's novel *Brideshead Revisited*. Waugh wrote the novel during the Second World War and confessed that war-time conditions had given him a craving for exotic luxuries. His description, therefore, of the rooms at Oxford decorated by the protagonist of the novel, Charles Ryder, on going up in the early 1920s, is a somewhat jaded one. Nonetheless, Charles Ryder's enthusiasms are not to be discounted by Waugh's mordant account:

I should like to think – indeed I sometimes do think – that I decorated those rooms with Morris stuffs and Arundel prints and that my shelves were filled with seventeenth century folios and French novels of the second empire in Russia-leather and watered silk. But this was not the truth. On my first afternoon I proudly hung a reproduction of van Gogh's *Sunflowers* over the fire and set up a screen, painted by Roger Fry with a Provençal landscape, which I had bought inexpensively when the Omega Workshops were sold up. I displayed also a poster by McKnight Kauffer and Rhyme Sheets from the Poetry Bookshop, and, most painful to recall, a porcelain figure of Polly Peachum which stood between black tapers on the chimney-piece. My books were meagre and commonplace – Roger Fry's *Vision and Design*, the Medici Press edition of *A Shropshire Lad*, *Eminent Victorians*, some volumes of *Georgian Poetry*, *Sinister Street* and *South Wind*. . . .[4]

Eminent Victorians 1921 Book jacket

Admirers of Kauffer will forgive this disparaging passage on the strength of the ironic precision with which Waugh locates early twenties aestheticism in the process of discarding it for nineties aestheticism. When Waugh designed the frontispiece for his novel *Vile Bodies* (1930) his design was definitely School of McKnight Kauffer.[5] The passage is richer in information on Kauffer's standing than might at first meet the eye. As well as the poster, which Ryder/Waugh could have bought from the Underground for a shilling or two, the copy of *Eminent Victorians* probably had the jacket designed by Kauffer just before he left for America. Among the Rhyme Sheets might have been Sacheverell Sitwell's poem 'The Parrot' – with decorations by Kauffer. The Rhyme Sheets and the volumes of *Georgian Verse* were published by Kauffer's friend Harold Monro of the Poetry Bookshop, who often went to another friend of Kauffer's, Gerard Meynell of the Westminster Press, for his printing. Roger Fry's *Vision and Design* completes the scene. Kauffer was already well on the way to becoming the dominant design influence in England of the inter-war period.

SOME CLIENTS: GERARD MEYNELL

Kauffer did not minimize the importance of his clients. Writing of poster advertising he acknowledged that designers were no more important

Gerard Meynell (about 1920)

Oldlands Mill, Ditchling 1917
Water-colour

Westminster Press 1922 Poster

ABC of Wines 1924

than 'the purchaser . . . who, seeing eye to eye with the designer, puts his convictions to the test of the hoarding itself'. With a retrospective glance he added, 'the hoardings of England today show more of this adventuresome spirit than do those of America, where new advances are supposed to be as welcome as central heating in winter'. In Gerard Meynell he found a pugnacious ally, as Frank Pick had done earlier. Gerard Tuke Meynell (1872–1944) came into printing from banking, and was a distant cousin of Francis Meynell. Gerard Meynell's work at the Westminster Press from 1900–31 was exemplary of the transition from the standards of nineties private press printing into the mainstream of commercial work.[6] It was also Gerard Meynell who had persuaded a reluctant Edward Johnston to accept Pick's commission for the Underground's new alphabet; Gerard Meynell again who had persuaded members of the Senefelder Club, an association of artist-lithographers, to design Underground posters for Pick in 1913. The Kauffers had known Gerard Meynell since 1917 when they went on a painting expedition to Ditchling, beside the South Downs in Sussex. This is the date of one of Kauffer's finest early water-colours, *Oldlands Mill, Ditchling*, which he inscribed to Meynell. It was on the same visit that the Kauffers met the sculptor and type designer Eric Gill, whose Gill Sans type-face Kauffer was to make good use of in the 1930s. Grace Kauffer was quietly impressed when she visited Gill's studio and noticed the little shrine to the Virgin where the sculptor always kept a lighted taper – only to be quietly shocked, in turn, when she saw Gill imperturbably lean over to the shrine to revive his pipe.

Meynell recognized that printing skills, especially in colour lithography, were being persistently wasted through poor creative talent. His magazine *The Imprint* (1913), a model of typographical clarity and elegance, charged that 'We see around us high technical skill, but almost no culture or taste. The artistic possibilities of lithography are scarcely realized by the public or the trade.' For example, the banal pantomime posters designed for Bovril by H.H. Harris or Septimus Scott misdirected lavish technical craftsmanship of great potential. Pleasant enough as Bovril posters were, they were also an abuse of six- or eight-colour lithography. Kauffer's simplifications were both aesthetically and practically an advance. Meynell took Kauffer on at the Westminster Press, after the American trip, as Director of Pictorial and Poster Advertising. Kauffer's poster for the Press used simple stripes in purple, red and orange – a scheme possibly derived from Ballet Russe designs – which set off the trade-mark of the Press, contributed by Gill. The mark includes a harrow – a neat reference to the address of the firm's works in the Harrow Road and presumably an indication of Meynell's reforming intentions. Kauffer also designed bright and economical publicity cards for the sister-company Sun Engraving.

An *ABC of Wines* published in 1924 is typical of Kauffer's association with Meynell. This was a rhyming wine list for Francis Downman of Dean Street ('whose wines are even better than his rhymes') –

> A is for ABSINTHE: let it alone.
> B is for big-bodied, blood-making BEAUNE.
> COCKTAILS are nice: but I honestly think
> Whoever takes cocktails is taking to drink (etc., etc.) –

but it was also a type specimen list for the Press and each line showed off a different type-face. Other productions were posters for 'Pomeroy Skin

Food' and an inventive series of press advertisements with Kauffer drawings for Shell. Francis Meynell was also designing witty press advertisements for Shell and others at his Pelican Press. The Underground quickly commissioned layouts from the Francis Meynell-Kauffer team. These bristled with new, newly imported or newly revived typefaces, set off by Kauffer's hand-drawn ornaments.

POSTERS FOR THE UNDERGROUND: THE 'MUSEUM' SET

On his return from New York Kauffer resumed work on a set of posters commissioned by Pick to advertise the principal museums in London. Some of these suggest a new range of influences that Kauffer began to channel into his work. A 1921 poster for the 'London Museum of Practical Geology' (now the Geology Museum, plate 15), continues Kauffer's streamlined Vorticist style. To illustrate his poster for the London Museum (plate 5) Kauffer chose the Great Fire of 1666. He may well have been turning this over in his mind when he wrote his article for *Arts and Decoration*, with its notes on colour and symbolic effect. Whether his ideas were influenced by Edward Wadsworth or not, his design for this poster seems to have been. The hint on which he based his poster may have been a few centimetres of curling flames in Wadsworth's woodcut *Black Country, Blast Furnace* (1918). The presumption is supported not only by a general similarity in the treatment of flames, but by the facts that – although usually printed only in black ink on white paper – Wadsworth also printed copies on orange paper (the predominant colour in Kauffer's poster), and finally that Kauffer himself owned a copy of the two-colour Wadsworth print. It is worth stressing such a derivation to give an idea of how Kauffer transformed slight hints into large-scale designs. This was also Kauffer's finale as a Vorticist.

A very different note is struck in his poster, also dated 1922, for London's Science Museum. This illustrates 'Mr Stephenson and his Rocket' and was based on the museum's miniaturized push-button display of George Stephenson's prototype steam locomotive. A historicist general flavour to the design is compounded by a direct affinity with a precise historical source. Kauffer seems to have been looking at Georgian trade-cards. A scroll of curling engine smoke containing lettering might actually be a translation into twenties idiom of the elegant engraved cartouches common to trade cards of the eighteenth century. Kauffer also prepared an alternative design for the Science Museum poster which survives in the form of a gouache 'rough'. This continues his Vorticist ideas: but either he or Pick had had enough and the milder neo-Georgian scheme was the one printed.

SOME CLIENTS: EASTMAN & CO LTD

A series of posters commissioned by Cyril Eastman for his dry-cleaning firm was also characterized by a pastiche, period flavour, in which Kauffer drew on period costume design and open-faced Regency type designs and mixed them up with jazzy decorative borders. The series appeared on the walls of Underground stations from 1921–6. Kauffer preserved all his life the gratifying sticker issued by Eastman's on an occasion when there was a production gap between two of his posters for their campaign. The sticker read: A NEW POSTER BY E. MCKNIGHT KAUFFER WILL BE SHOWN HERE SHORTLY.[7] There is little hard information on Kauffer's commercial effectiveness in advertising, whatever his public acclaim. One poster for Eastman's was reported in a

Black Country, Blast Furnace 1918
Woodcut by Edward Wadsworth

Science Museum 1922 Poster

Science Museum 1922 Alternative design

Gloves Cleaned 1923 Poster

trade paper to have increased orders for glove-cleaning from 9000 to 15,000 pairs a week.[8]

SOME RESPONSES TO KAUFFER'S WORK

A casual reference to the banality of posters issued by Pear's Soap, made in passing by a writer in the *London Mercury* in 1921, occasioned an angry and tautological reply:

Impossible ducks, futurist trees, vermilion grass, and such like absurdities may appeal to what, as I have no wish to be offensive, I will call the 'higher thought', but believe me, Sir, those people who live their lives in the ordinary, conventional way, as do the bulk of the general public, need nothing more subtle in a poster than a straightforward appeal to their sense of pleasure, duty, or whatever it may be. They don't understand, and have no wish to understand, the essentially unacademic.[9]

This riposte came from S. Bernard Smith, advertising manager of Pear's. The company's notorious *Bubbles* poster, the Millais painting doctored to include a bar of Pear's Soap, was still selling 10,000 copies a year. The Design and Industries Association arranged a meeting two years later to discuss quality in poster advertising.[10] Kauffer spoke and his statement follows the general lines of an article he published a year later as 'The Poster and Symbolism'. He described himself as designing for a fast-moving public and spoke of his use of symbols:

Daily new devices are invented which the designer can develop into a symbol. The aeroplane, for example, would, if we used signs as a means of communication, convey to us speed, travel, an engine of war and terror, as well as aspiration on the part of man to be as a bird.[11]

Bernard Smith replied at the meeting that the public was not interested in such things and even that 'there was an antipathy to new design and colour itself'. A report of the proceedings goes on: 'Mr Smith had only discovered that evening that Mr Kauffer's latest Eastman poster was not a lampshade, but a dress such as the wife of no member present would wear.' These humdrum sallies were followed up by the invention 'McKnightmare' in a trade journal. On the other hand, Kauffer was chosen to design eight of the posters for the different pavilions at the British Empire Exhibition at Wembley in 1924. He was unlucky not to have been given the commission to design the British lion which symbolized the event. This went to F.C. Herrick, whose design is very close in stylization to that of one of Kauffer's most widely seen inventions. This was the crowing cock he designed for Eno's Fruit Salt ('The Effervescent Saline', plate 19) in 1924. The company were pleased with the success of the poster, which was also used as a full-page colour advertisement, and sent Kauffer a cheque for £50 on top of his original fee.[12] As a non-national Kauffer may have been thought an inappropriate choice for the British Empire symbol and he was not included in the British pavilion at the Paris Exhibition of decorative and industrial arts in 1925. As Britain's major graphic exponent of the style named from the exhibition, 'Art Deco', he was unlucky not to have been included. There was no American pavilion.

The official general report found the entry of British posters to be faulted by prolixity of detail and lack of clarity in presentation. The art critic of *The Times* patriotically stood up for British design and said that the British Section was simply not well chosen:

There is nothing in their respective kinds being better done anywhere on the Continent than the pottery of Mr W. Staite Murray and Mr Bernard Leach, the weaving of Mrs Mairet, the furniture of Mr Gordon Russell, and the posters of Mr E. McKnight Kauffer.[13]

This was good company for Kauffer to be in. French book illustration and theatre design, together with painting and poster design, became increasingly influential in his work in the mid-twenties. He also made a fateful visit to Paris in the summer of 1923. The Kauffers were about to leave for Paris when a quarrel broke out. Kauffer went on his own. In Paris he met Marion Dorn, a designer from California whom he had first encountered in New York in 1921. He returned to London with her and repeated the pattern of his own childhood by leaving his wife and young child. Kauffer and Marion Dorn lived together unmarried until 1950, when they were eventually married in City Hall, New York. Grace Kauffer brought up her daughter, Ann, with great hardship. She did not have the opportunity to continue her career as a concert pianist but over the years, as Grace McKnight, trained many young soloists.[14]

NEW NOTES IN DESIGN: JAZZ AND ARCHAISM

'What will become of those stern and grandly plastic glimpses of a novel universe, which first saw the light in the Western capitals immediately before the war, it is impossible to say', Wyndham Lewis wrote in 1937.[15] He recognized that, although 'one Kauffer does not make an Underground summer', Vorticism had had a general influence on design. By 1923 Kauffer had exhausted the immediate possibilities of the style and was adopting a new range of interests:

It seems at the moment that the designer must contemplate his 'modernism'. In itself it is an excellent accomplishment, and in the service of advertising psychologically of importance. It has, or should have, increased the scope of one's invention, so that the newer devices of mankind could be incorporated as symbols or motives for the designer's use. But like everything else, the 'new' spirit in design must grow to continue to be of use. Growth is more often a matter of going back to reconstruct from the past, which in itself stabilises the tentative suggestions coming from the designer. He is a link between old and new, and the results of his experiments can be analysed and found to be correct according to the traditional principles. In turning back the designer finds that the architecture of design has few 'ground plans', but many varieties of edifices have been and can be built upon these perhaps limited outlines. In the latter the designer displays his individuality, while in the former he can but use what is his by right of understanding.[16]

A second glance at Charles Ryder's Oxford rooms shows that Waugh had caught that retrospective note well too – in the Polly Peachum figure, the archaizing lyric poems of Housman, and the volumes of *Georgian Poetry* – one of which borrowed a puce colour for its cover from *Blast* but decorated its title-page with seventeenth-century printer's flowers. Kauffer himself noted that 'the tendency of press and periodical advertisement today is toward the sedate title page of years past, and because of this the designer should know the earlier forms, and should as well be familiar with the best type-founts'.[17] Forgotten type-faces were at that moment not only being revived in press layouts but more significantly being adapted for modern printing through Stanley Morison and the Monotype Corporation. Kauffer's typographer friends Francis Meynell and Gerard Meynell were also active in this reclamation of traditional type designs.

Another immediate source for this mood in Kauffer's work was Harold Monro, poetaster, publisher of the Rhyme Sheets – based on

Poetry Bookshop sign 1926

The Chinese Conjuror 1917
Picasso costume design

traditional broadside ballad sheets and intended to find a new and wider audience for verse – and proprietor of the Poetry Bookshop. Kauffer contributed drawings to Monro's journal *The Chap Book*, including a portrait of Monro and illustrations to T.S. Eliot's poem 'Doris's Dream Songs'.[18] In 1926 Kauffer designed a painted sign-board for the Poetry Bookshop when it moved to new premises at 38 Great Russell Street, opposite the British Museum. Typically of Kauffer's mid-twenties style, the sign-board is a jazzy interpretation of traditional devices. Its dominant scarlet colouring would have been intended to pick up the red window surrounds and red interior of the shop. By this time, however, beige and cream were part of Kauffer's range of colours and these began a further transition in his work which belongs to the next chapter.[19]

In 1924 Kauffer published his book *The Art of the Poster*, which he dedicated to Frank Pick. The title on the cover is set in Johnston Sans. Among friends Kauffer thanked for their help in making the book were Harold Monro and Gerard Meynell and the printers were Westminster Press. The book includes a historical note on posters by R.A. Stephens and theoretical notes by Phillips Russell. Kauffer provided passages of exemplary formal analysis of a number of the plates. The illustrations included the historical and ecumenical: Greek vase drawings, Byzantine mosaics, Chinese stone reliefs, medieval brass rubbings, Chinese and Japanese woodcuts, eighteenth-century trade cards, nineteenth-century broadsides, and historical and contemporary posters. Kauffer himself owned a number of posters illustrated in the book, including examples by Toulouse-Lautrec, Cheret, Beardsley, the Russians Stelletski and Soudekeine, and Picasso. Of these only the Picasso, a costume design of 1917 for *Parade*, which Kauffer captioned as having been used as a poster advertising the Russian Ballet 'when in England', seems to have a direct bearing on Kauffer's posters of this period. At the time he was active as a set and costume designer for the Arts League of Service Travelling Theatre.[20] Little evidence of his work for the ALS survives but the Picasso poster provides a clue to the major source of Kauffer's next important set of posters.

In 1925 the Underground published three 'Summer' posters by Kauffer.[21] The trio resembles a triptych – a large central panel flanked by two smaller subjects (plates 36–38). However, the large poster called *Summertime in the Country* was shown in station vestibules and corridors, while the smaller ones flanked station entrances. The group together forms one of Kauffer's most splendid sets. The symmetry of the landscape of *Summertime in the Country* was said at the time to symbolize summer.[22] Kauffer might have seen symmetrical landscapes in Indian paintings when he designed a poster for the Indian Museum in 1924. A more obvious source, however, would be in theatre design. His poster suggests a proscenium arch and theatre backdrop.

One of the smaller posters represents *Jack i' the Green*, a fertility king from English folklore, who appears on May Day dressed in green leaves and persists as the 'somerkyng'. The crown he wears in Kauffer's poster is not dissimilar to the head-dress of the Chinese conjuror in Picasso's poster, and the sunburst behind it is suggestive of the sun which adorns another costume Picasso designed for *Parade*, this time for the Acrobat. Jack i' the Green's costume, on the other hand, derives – appropriately enough – from the 'folklorique' costumes of Bakst, Goncharova and Tchelitchew. These assimilate peasant motifs to a sophisticated geometric style. The third poster shows *Summertime in the Town* – a Pierrot playing a guitar among parked circus caravans. The background again suggests a theatrical *mise en scène* and the Pierrot is perhaps less a direct borrowing from Picasso's *Pulcinella* (1920) than the generalized figure of the Noel Coward lyric 'Parisian pierrot (what makes you so blue?)'. The Ballet Russe performed, during their 1924 London season, in a novel context – as part of a Variety programme at the Coliseum. This link between avant-garde and popular elements was furthered by Kauffer's posters, which gave a sparkling rendition of the style at street level.

WORK IN THE THEATRE

Kauffer's early experience of travelling theatres was put to good use by the Arts League of Service, which regarded its travelling theatre as its most important activity. Kauffer designed a poster for the travelling theatre and sets and costumes for *The Man who Married a Dumb Wife* by Anatole France. The plays toured all over Britain in a converted Lancia van – venues included Borstal reformatories as well as theatres.[23] Kauffer also designed sets and costumes for productions of the Incorporated Stage Society – *The Rumour* by C.K. Munro at the Globe Theatre in 1922, *Progress* by C.K. Munro at the New Theatre in 1924, *The Colonnade* by Stark Young at the Aldwych Theatre in 1925. He seems to have had a little more success with a production by A.E. Filmer and Ernest Milton of Pirandello's *Henry IV* at the Everyman Theatre in Hampstead, for which he designed 'Stage Decorations' and Marion Dorn designed costumes. *Vogue* published a photograph of Ernest Milton as *Henry IV*, holding a long silk length printed by Marion Dorn with her own abstract design.[24] Such scarce records of Kauffer's early theatre work as survive suggest that the *Summertime* posters are a fair guide.

Henry VIII (about 1925)
Costume design for ALS

THE ANATOMY OF MELANCHOLY

At this period Kauffer was a close friend of Francis Meynell, from whom he rented a studio at 16 Great James Street in Bloomsbury. The office of Meynell's Nonesuch Press was next door and he recalled that Kauffer was 'a romantic theorist about art and there was more discussion between us than work. Admired as he was, his was not so lucrative a success as to make it easy for him always to pay his quarter's rent. No matter; for I had made a bargain with him that whenever he began a sentence with the words "The Artist" he was to pay me half-a-crown spot cash. This more than sufficed to clear the arrears.'[25] Kauffer was fond of quoting lavishly and often from Robert Burton's *The Anatomy of Melancholy*. Burton's remark that 'literature is high-born stealth' would, transposed to poster design, admirably describe Kauffer's adaptive-creative method. For Meynell, as he later wrote:

Kauffer was an example of the abandoned truth that art is indivisible: that the man with the root of the matter in him can paint or design rugs or make posters or illustrate books or decorate a room or parti-colour a motor-car or scheme an advertisement with the best of the over-specialists.[26]

Certainly in 1925 Kauffer designed an 'Art Deco' office for the advertising agent T.B. Lawrence,[27] turned to rug designing in 1929, had already 'schemed' press advertisements with Meynell, designed the jacket for Meynell's first edition of that typical twenties production *The Weekend Book* (Kauffer's motif picks up the title of Harold Monro's prefatory poem 'The Train') – and he did also parti-colour Meynell's car. Unfortunately no photograph was taken of this – but if, as seems likely, it was in Kauffer's 'jazz' style it must have been spectacular. Kauffer

The Week End Book 1924 Book jacket

Office for T.B. Lawrence (about 1925)

batiked a purple and puce silk evening dress for Esther Meynell in 1924.[28] Francis Meynell commissioned from Kauffer his first illustrated book – perhaps inevitably, Burton's *Anatomy*. Meynell recalled in 1955:

When last I saw him he told me that he still kept something like forty letters of mine, letters nagging, beseeching, criticizing and praising the drawings as they came singly or in batches, with long gaps, over many months, months during which his own art so changed that the early drawings and the late have little in common. What a pity that only the worthless end of our correspondence survives![29]

The volumes of Burton suggest a close relationship between illustrator and typographer in the matching of text, image and format. The book is a good example of Kauffer's interest in erecting new edifices on 'old ground plans'. The title-page neatly updated Christof Le Blon's engraved title-page for the 5th edition published in 1638. The weight of the emphatically hatched line drawings is balanced by Meynell's choice of Plantin – robust as well as elegant – for the type-face. The weight and simplicity of stylization suggest an origin for Kauffer's style in Paris,

The Anatomy of Melancholy
Title pages, 1638 and 1925
and page 331

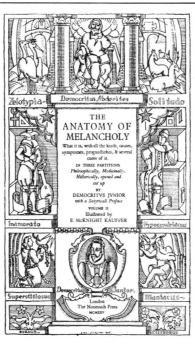

possibly using hints from Derain, Georges Laboureur and perhaps distantly from the Neo-Classicism of Picasso. Roger Fry aptly defined the style as a 'cubistico-cabbalistic mixture'. (The mixture includes a dash of Surrealism.) Fry was alive to the qualities of the whole production:

The general effect of an ancient portfolio is preserved without any affected archaism, all is clear, lucid, well planned and admirably printed on very good paper. Mr Kauffer has clearly appreciated these qualities in his drawings. He has determined that in every way they should conform to the general effect of 'colour' of the printed page. This means that he has had to maintain a certain average density of tone in his drawings, nowhere allowing too heavy or too closely placed darks, and nowhere becoming so thin as to leave a 'hole' in the page.[30]

Fry also found Kauffer's illustrative commentary on Burton's allusive, rambling, pseudo-scientific prose entirely apt. Kauffer's playful use of Cubist devices combined 'pseudo-scientific witticism' and 'pseudo-archaistic pedantry'. Kauffer rarely designed a humorous poster: his 150 drawings for *The Anatomy of Melancholy* are the best graphic evidence for his genuine vein of whimsical wit. Fry exactly pinpointed Kauffer's spirit of 'affectionate raillery':

He must enjoy Burton's flavour to the full, but he is guilty of no ill manners if, after all these centuries, he now and then takes us, rather than the author, into his confidence; if he now and then whispers to us in a voice which the old man cannot overhear, 'Isn't he a delightful old buffer? Let's keep him at it!'

RETROSPECTIVE EXHIBITION OF POSTERS 1925

Almost comically, Burton closed his enormous and convoluted tome with a very plain final precept indeed: 'Be not solitary, be not idle.' It is clear that Kauffer's gifts included two that were important for his career: a gift for friendship and a gift for hard work. His crowded year, 1925, was crowned by a Retrospective Exhibition of his posters of the previous 10 years. Fifty-six posters were shown at the exhibition, which was arranged by the Arts League of Service at 60 Gower Street, Bloomsbury, in May and June. In addition Kauffer showed original drawings, first drafts, colour schemes, a selection of calendars, show-cards, labels, book-jackets, drawings for newspaper advertisements, and ten stage-proofs showing the lithographic printing of his poster *Hadley Wood* by Vincent, Brooks, Day & Son. The ALS chose the occasion to announce the opening of a 'Poster Bureau', in collaboration with Kauffer. This was intended 'to secure the work of the younger artists for the advertising world by finding them an immediate outlet for their work'. A note in the catalogue of the exhibition states that Kauffer's larger posters could not be displayed because of lack of space – specifically, the *Back to Methuselah* and *He Who Gets Slapped* posters for Theatre Guild, and the eight sectional posters for the British Empire Exhibition.

Roger Fry provided an introduction to the catalogue, reviewed the exhibition in *The Nation* on 23 May and, when the exhibition was afterwards shown at the Ashmolean Museum, Oxford, gave a lecture on *Commerce and Art*. The lecture was revised and subsequently published as a pamphlet by the Hogarth Press.[31] Fry spoke critically of the 'romantic' images built up through advertising by railway companies which 'give us progressively worse and worse accommodation', and induce the loyalty of a public they simply exploit. Was Kauffer's work, then, gilt on stale gingerbread? Clough Williams-Ellis, a critic no less astringent than Fry, wrote more favourably of at least one railway company in his 'Material Review' column in the *Spectator* in 1923:

When the old Metropolitan Railway exchanged steam amd smoke for electricity and grimy brickwork for gleaming tiles, it also set up a new standard of civic decency and established a lead in commercial efficiency that it still maintains.[32]

Certainly for Frank Pick every detail was of importance. Fry continued:

What is interesting to me in this new business is that I see a possibility of commerce doing something to redress the balance in favour of art – that balance which it so ruthlessly upset in the other direction by driving all artists out of the business of designing for the textiles, pottery, etc., of ordinary use. For the poster is not a very expensive object. It is possible here for the industrialist to take risks which he would never take in setting up a textile design, or a design for linoleum, or for any of the objects of large-scale production.

The cost of a print-run of 1500 Underground posters at this date was about £25 – say, the price of one painting by a reasonably well-known artist. The designer's fee was probably at about the same level. In addition, Fry pointed out, poster art was 'a new medium without preconceptions', with 'no fixed and traditional notion of the kind of thing a poster ought to be':

There is as yet no pedantry, no culture, no lecturing, until tonight, to hamper and harness the man who happens to have a gift for expression in this medium. For all these reasons the art of poster design holds out opportunities of a kind that are all too rare in modern life. This exhibition tells me how far they have been realized.

Other critics agreed, from R.R. Tatlock in the *Burlington Magazine* to Raymond Mortimer who wrote an unsigned profile of Kauffer for *Vogue*'s 'Hall of Fame' page. 1925 marks the climax of Kauffer's early period as a designer. The second half of the decade saw his enthusiastic amateurism shade towards a new professionalism.

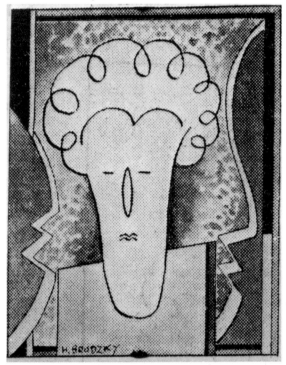

Kauffer 'drawn in his own style' by Horace Brodzky,
News Chronicle 1931

Chapter 4. **The Late Twenties**

THERE ARE remarkably few stories or anecdotes about Kauffer. Even the Poet Laureate Sir John Betjeman, who must receive many appeals for such information – and signed his letter of reply 'Archivist to the late twenties' – admitted that

There is nothing that I can add to all that has been written about that great and good man. He was one of those mild, gentle people on whom everyone ambitious, such as I, imposed. I am sure that it was out of the goodness of his heart that he did the dust-wrapper of *Continual Dew*. . . .[1]

As well as that jacket for the Laureate's first book, Kauffer provided the title-page for the first volume published by another Oxford aesthete of the Betjeman-Waugh vintage – *Cornelian* by Harold Acton. Acton's *Memoirs of an Aesthete* provides a rare close-up view of Kauffer and Marion Dorn when they lived in a flat in the Adelphi in the late twenties:

Ted's flat was all beige and aluminium, ultra-modern, austere yet comfortable with discreet lighting and the latest gadgets. . . . Marion's modernist rugs kept one's eyes riveted to the floor. Their work detained them in town when they longed for the country, for they were superstitious about physical fitness and fancied that the London air was noxious. They should have been nudists, playing in the sunshine, but some ingrained puritanism held them in check.[2]

Acton also noticed Kauffer's restless drive for work:

he had hitched his wagon to sone unattainable star, for he was morose and misanthropic. People sapped his energy, and the attractive, sociable Marion had the irksome duty of keeping them away.

Continual Dew 1937 Book jacket

Cornelian 1928 Frontispiece

Sir Stephen Tallents (about 1930)

This is an interesting view of Kauffer, whom most people found gentle, generous and charming. Acton's description of the flat is a valuable document as Kauffer's living quarters were always fastidiously designed. It was probably this flat, according to Douglas Cleverdon (who had the distinction of initiating the prototype of Eric Gill's famous Gill Sans type-face) 'a masterpiece of modern interior design', which Kauffer was obliged by the landlord to restore to its original state when he left it. Photographs of one or another of Kauffer's flats of the twenties may survive but at present their whereabouts is unknown. The beige and aluminium recorded by Acton neatly suggests the style of the later twenties and Kauffer's role, supported by the 'gadgetry', less as 'artist in advertising' more as professional designer. The main theme of this chapter is a growing institutionalization of his role.

THE EMPIRE MARKETING BOARD 1926–33

The Empire Marketing Board, the E.M.B., was an ambitious new departure into mass communications made by the British government. The purpose of the Board was to create favourable market conditions for Empire and Home produce. The electorate had in the 1923 general election rejected proposals to raise tariffs against foreign produce. The E.M.B. was to be an exercise in persuasion, to establish a mass preference for Empire produce by appeals to loyalty, solidarity and interest. In a nutshell, the agency saw its task as 'to bring alive the idea of Empire'. The interpretation of the Board's function was very much influenced by its Secretary, and Civil Service head, Stephen Tallents. Presumably without any ironic intention, *The Times* titled his obituary simply 'An Imaginative Civil Servant'.[3] Tallents's colleague Gervas Huxley recalled meeting him when the E.M.B. was founded:

He was in his early forties, a trim military figure, spare, balding, and moving briskly with a limp, the legacy of a severe wound at Festubert in 1915. Radiating confidence and energy, he spoke of his new job with contagious enthusiasm.[4]

Tallents's distinguished career had included the Governorship of the Baltic port of Riga during a period of emergency. He regarded the E.M.B. as 'an early response to a demand more catholic and more penetrating than the need to promote the marketing of Empire products'.[5] He saw it as pioneering mass communications in a mass society, and recognized value in the way such a society explains itself to itself. The major and widely admired achievement of the Board was in documentary film. John Grierson's *Drifters* 1929 is its classic. Grierson's documentary film fulfils his demand that 'the affairs of our time should be brought to the screen in any fashion which strikes the imagination, and makes observation a little richer than before'.[6] The poetics of realism in his work is defined by contrast with a film of much the same date. Anthony Asquith made *Underground* (1928) for British Instructional Films – but if they saw it neither Grierson nor Frank Pick can have been happy with the result. Instead of finding interest in the actual running of a complex mass transportation system, Asquith superimposed on the facts a banal love story and *crime passionel* involving scuffles in lifts and bloody clamberings over turbines in power stations. Sentimentality overlaid a complex subject which might itself have proved to have dramatic potential on film. In contrast to this Tallents quoted with approval some remarks of Walt Whitman's, from his *Backward Glance O'er Travel'd Roads*, which proved to be a widespread inspiration for the documentary movement: 'Whatever may have been the case in years gone by, the true use of the imaginative faculty of modern times is to give ultimate vivification to facts, to science, and to common lives, endowing them with the glows and glories and final illustriousness which belongs to every real thing and to real things only.'[7]

An international outlook at the E.M.B. is registered in the influence from Russia in the film unit, while Tallents immediately recognized the German contribution to exhibition design. Of Mies van der Rohe's German pavilion at Barcelona in 1929 Tallents wrote:

One feels in this pavilion the expression of a lonely, powerful and forward-looking spirit – a gesture, incomplete in itself, which was fulfilled in the displays of German industry elsewhere in the Exhibition.[8]

Kauffer shared this internationalism of outlook, and it is appropriate to make a connection between him and the documentary film-makers. With his friend Sidney Bernstein and others Kauffer founded the Film Society in London in 1925 – a principal channel through which England became aware of modern experimental film (and which premiered *Drifters* in 1929). Lord Bernstein recalls that Kauffer 'was persuaded to design the monogram for the Society – a much admired, bold FS with a tiny attenuated figure attached, deciphered variously as a Cupid and as a Red Indian'.[9] One of the ambitions of X Group had been to design for the film industry. In 1926 Kauffer made a poster design for the Fritz Lang film *Metropolis* – perhaps on speculation (it was never used).[10] Film continued to fascinate him and in the thirties he talked of making a series of films with Aldous Huxley on such subjects as dreams and 'Types' (presumably printing types).[11] His one graphic contribution to film history was his collaboration with Ivor Montagu, another Film Society associate, on the titles of Alfred Hitchcock's feature *The Lodger*

Film Society symbol 1925

Main title for *The Lodger* 1926

(1926). Kauffer's designs came about in the following way, as Ivor Montagu has explained:

The film had been more or less completed by Hitchcock, but, like the latter's two previous films was held up by the distributor who disliked or pretended to dislike it. M.E. Balcon (now Sir Michael), the producer (as Gainsborough Pictures) of the film asked me – who had never previously done any commercial work but

Title for *The Lodger* 1926

whom he knew from the Film Society – if I would look at it with a view to
re-editing it. His idea was: if the film was too highbrow for the distributor,
perhaps it was spoiled by not being presented 'highbrow'. I undertook the job
and because I admired Kauffer's graphic work so much, and partly, possibly,
following out the same sequence of ideas, asked him to view the film and work
out with me backgrounds for the titles (rewriting of which of course was part of
the re-editing). This he did with readiness and enthusiasm, and no doubt
contributed thereby, as we all had hoped, to the singularity of the treatment of
the whole and so to its success.[12]

Kauffer's punchy titles, using the bold Neuland display type-face,
sustain the strength and dramatic tension of the narrative. An
introductory title sets the scene for Hitchcock's menacing 'tale of the
London fog'. Kauffer's proposal for the film poster, however, was
rejected by the distributor as being 'too artistic' – surprisingly in view of
the film's adaptation 'upmarket'.[13]

Tallents formed a Poster Sub-Committee at the E.M.B. and appointed
to it Frank Pick and Sir William Crawford, head of Crawford's
Advertising Agency. Tallents later described the committee meetings in
his still unpublished book on the E.M.B., *Empire Experiment*:

A small group under Pick's chairmanship used to meet at night, week after
week, when the ordinary office day was ended, to devise new themes, to choose
the artist to which each should be entrusted, to talk over its treatment with the
chosen artist and later to discuss and sometimes to criticize first his roughs and
then his finished designs. Pick was accustomed to commission artists. Some of
them, he knew, must be left to follow their own inspirations. But many, he
knew also, gain by having definite subjects suggested to them, provided that
those subjects are suited to their talents, and that each man is left free, once a
theme and its general treatment had been agreed, to pursue the idea in his own
manner and style. Sometimes we thought him a bit dogmatic in his handling of
the men and women who would come in succession with their portfolios to sit
with us at those evening meetings round the table of our modest board room in
Queen Anne's Gate Buildings. Now and then, I felt, we damped a man's
enthusiasm and lost something in the quality of his work. But in the main those
late night meetings secured the delivery of the goods we wanted.[14]

This account suggests that Pick was no soft touch as a buyer of design
and in the next decade even Kauffer had his disagreements with him.

The poster campaign opened with a special one-day exhibition at the Royal Academy on 2 November 1926, which was held for the benefit of delegates from Empire countries, and for the press. A pair of tropical scenes by Kauffer, *Cocoa* and *Bananas* – which successfully used an Art Deco style to represent exotic lands – were regarded as the outstanding designs.[15] They appeared on the hoardings in autumn 1927 under the title 'Half the Empire in the Tropics'. The design of the hoardings themselves was considered (a typical Pick touch). They were to be special and used only for E.M.B. posters. Hoardings were constructed in English oak and British Columbian pine and by the end of 1928 occupied nearly 1000 sites around the country which were given free or at peppercorn rents.[16] In design these hoardings were again distinct because they were divided into five panels: either two large ones below, three smaller ones above, or a horizontal sequence. Pictorial posters – like Kauffer's tropical set – were placed in the larger panels (40 × 60 inches in size). The central panel above was used for a main title and flanked by letterpress information at the wings. The Publicity Committee at the E.M.B. recommended that the Board restrict itself to posters of 'real artistic value. It is thought that such work makes a deeper and more arresting appeal to the public than ordinary commercial work while being more in consonance with the character of the Board's campaign.'[17]

Kauffer's *Tropical* set on an E.M.B. hoarding 1927

The campaign opened with a world map by Macdonald Gill. Copies 10 × 20 feet in size were shown at Piccadilly Circus and Charing Cross. William Nicholson, half of the great 'Beggarstaff Brothers' poster partnership of the 1890s, contributed a five-section poster on Empire Children. Other commissions included a set on English orchards by John and Paul Nash, a modernist industrial series by Clive Gardiner, a trio of still-life oil paintings by Mark Gertler (which proved too expensive in colour printing and were not used) and, more adventurously, a set of industrial scenes titled 'Peace' by Stanley Spencer. The Publicity Committee regarded Spencer's work as too provocative and his designs were never used – to Pick's fury, which abated to some extent when he sold them to a dealer at slight profit to the Board. The Board was, in fact, attacked for its policy by the British Poster Advertising Association, which issued *Some Arguments and Suggestions Submitted to the Empire Marketing Board* in 1929. The Association was nettled because the Board spurned conventional hoardings. It also charged the E.M.B. with failure to 'appreciate the mass-mind':

Not only are the 'masses' – that is to say, the poorer 95% of the population – indifferent to good art, *but they do not understand it*. It is not that they fail to appreciate the merits of a good picture in the modernist style used by most of the Board's artists. *They don't know what these pictures are meant to represent!*

The pamphlet, for all its underlinings, cut no ice with the E.M.B. A series of 836 posters was completed in the Board's six years. Pick clearly dominated the campaign, which also utilized Johnston Sans. This remained the best Sans Serif display face until Eric Gill's Gill Sans became available from the Monotype Corporation in 1930. The E.M.B. hoped at one point to secure the new face for its exclusive use. In addition to its hoardings the Board distributed class-room size versions of its posters to a list of 27,000 schools.[18]

Kauffer's contributions to the E.M.B. included a lion symbol which was used on a large-scale 'message board' (16 sheets) in May 1927.[19] He also designed a 'National Mark' which identified British goods on

The Projection of England 1932
Book jacket

packaging and in advertising. There were three versions of this National Mark – one for England and Wales, one for Scotland, one for Ireland. Kauffer used this design as the basis of a cover he designed for Tallents's major public statement on mass-communications, *The Projection of England* 1932. Tallents published this pamphlet because by 1932 the future of the E.M.B. was already uncertain. His arguments were intended to prevent the dissolution of the Board, or at least to redeploy it as a national propaganda machine. *The Times* published an article by Tallents under the same title on 16 April 1932. The authorities were not moved and the E.M.B., which had always been disliked by bureaucracy, was dissolved in 1933. *The Projection of England* called for a 'school of national projection' and it was clearly based on Tallents's admiration for Soviet film-making of the twenties. He argued that the Soviet classic *Storm over Asia* could be outmatched by a British-made *Dawn over Africa*.

Tallents saw exhibition design as another under-developed resource. He argued for the creation of an organization which would operate with some of the authority of government and much of the freedom of free enterprise (anticipating the 'Quango' – quasi autonomous national government organization – of modern parlance). His team would be creative and experimental, entering fully 'into the ordinary life of their country, avoiding that instinct of withdrawal which has made the government services of the world the legitimate successors of the monastic orders'. Lord Clark suggests that Tallents never fully realized his talents, as he was obstructed by the Civil Service.[20] Another passage from his pamphlet is of interest because it shows the temper of one of Kauffer's key clients of the late twenties and the thirties:

Private art has become a luxury scarcely to be afforded and remote from our manner of living. Already the public patron is yearly superseding the private in the arts of architecture and decoration. The call is for the encouragement of a national rather than a private art, and the patron who gave that encouragement would know that he was not merely satisfying a noble taste but was fulfilling one of the great needs of his country.[21]

Tallents did not save the E.M.B., which was dissolved after the Ottawa Conference of Empire Nations in 1933. Tallents took some pleasure in being appointed the first 'Public Relations Officer' – a new phrase imported from America – appointed in the Civil Service when he joined the General Post Office in 1933. There he set about projecting England in spite of the Civil Service. His splendid ambitions match Kauffer's romantic idealism and their partnership continued in the next decade.

KAUFFER AT CRAWFORD'S 1927–9

The E.M.B. poster campaign had been Pick's Underground policy expanded, and was a lesser achievement than was effected in film. It was probably a useful step for Kauffer to join Sir William Crawford's agency, which – through its Berlin office Dorland's – was alive to continental developments in graphic design. Kauffer's two years' association with the firm prompted or coincided with large changes in his style. Perhaps more valuable than that, his presence there so impressed his colleagues that, through their memories, we have our first glimpse of Kauffer at work. He was brought into the firm by its dashing Art Director Ashley Havinden.[22] Ashley, as he was known as a designer, pooled his memories with those of Mr W. Hellicar, Kauffer's assistant at Crawford's, 45 years later.[23]

Kauffer's arrival had a revolutionary effect on Crawford's designers. While they sat at cramped work tables, Kauffer stood up at an adjustable architect's desk imported from Germany. He worked with plenty of space around him so that he could study his design from different angles as he developed it. Expensive long-handled brushes stood in readiness in a huge stone jar. While the other designers used Clifford and Millburn's poster paints and shiny white hot-pressed boards like starched collars, Kauffer used artist's materials: Newton's gouache and Ingres paper. Working in a standing position as he did, Kauffer had tailored for himself a special waistcoat which omitted the untidy strap at the back. He would test colours against each other from a hoard of coloured papers, with which he also made experimental shapes. Novel letter forms were cut out in brown paper. To achieve colours which were rich but not glaring he always passed them through a proportion of black. When he found a colour which satisfied him he would mix up a good quantity of it and keep it with others in a nest of ceramic paint dishes. A junior would keep these colours fresh by adding a drop of moisture to them each day. On a rack was a series of white enamelled butcher's trays on which designs could be placed and slid into the rack to dry. Beside him Kauffer kept a battery of flexible rulers, French curves and hinged triangles. The walls of his studio were painted in different tones of grey to achieve a diffused light.

His studio was high up in the building at 233 High Holborn designed for Crawford by Frederick Etchells (1927), itself a confident and elegant structure in the style of le Corbusier. Kauffer's studio was off the part called 'The Palace of Beauty', an old Victorian edifice encased in Etchells's streamlined new one. Here Kauffer worked under an arrangement which was probably for three days a week. He was always happier as a freelance but often took part-time positions such as this to provide the basis of his income. A designer of Kauffer's calibre would at this period have earned in the region of £3000 a year, averaging £50 for an individual poster design (at twenties monetary value).

The two years at Crawford's see an end to the 'Jazz and Archaism' flavour of Kauffer's style. Professionally and stylistically he became an arch-modernist. Photo-montage appears in his work for the first time, adapted from Russian and German examples. Rectangular layouts replace the dynamic diagonal movement of the earlier twenties. The sobriety of blue and brown colour schemes displaces Ballet Russe exuberance. Defying traditional typographic good taste, aluminium ink makes its appearance, and blocks of type-matter – no longer emulating 'the sedate title-page of years past' – are cavalierly crushed into parallelograms.

Typical of these developments is a brochure designed by Kauffer to promote the Chrysler 62 and 72 cars about 1928. A bronze-coloured ink was used for the cover, with lettering in terracotta and a symbol in dark blue. Each page opening is a variation of squares and circles printed in aluminium and royal blue, with text and diagrams in chocolate brown. The trick of using positive and negative lettering, which Kauffer first tried out in the Film Society symbol of 1925, became a favourite device. This habit of reversing lettering into light and dark as a word 'crosses over' broad rectangles of colour was a hallmark of Russian experimental graphics in the early twenties. The style reached Paris at least by 1923, when performances by the Moscow Chamber Theatre were advertised by a poster designed by Vladimir A. Stenberg which shows off the full repertoire of the style.[24] Photo-montage was in use at

Chrysler brochure (about 1928)

1929 photo-montage 1928–9

Phoenix Theatre symbol 1930

Crawford's at this period, and the agency produced a series of posters for Worthington's Beer which are entirely in this technique. Kauffer himself chose to counterpoint photographic quotation with areas of flat painted colour.

A new discipline also occurs in Kauffer's lettering, which was often the weakest part of his earlier designs, and all too obviously hand-made. To complete his conversion to a machine-made look to his work Kauffer took up the air-brush. In his early work Kauffer had mastered the art of 'feathering' paint so that one hue shades from full saturation to a diluted, paler, variant. The air-brush allowed such shadings to reach a mechanical exactness impossible to achieve by hand. Kauffer used it to suggest the softness of Kayser stockings and the smoothness of Bass ales. His interest in continental, particularly German, typography and graphics was reciprocated in May 1929 when his work was featured in *Gebrauchsgraphic* magazine. Published in this context Kauffer's work up to 1925 looks decidedly old-fashioned. His jazz style was over – by the time he designed a photo-montage emblem for the year 1929 he could include a jazz element simply by 'quoting' a photo of a line of dance-band saxophone players.[25] When a bird motif appeared once more in 1930 it had also passed through a radical revision. When Sidney Bernstein's Phoenix Theatre opened in 1930 (Noel Coward and Gertie Lawrence in the hit *Private Lives*) its symbol was Kauffer's – a silver phoenix among bronze flames.

BOOK ILLUSTRATIONS

The Nonesuch Press followed up the two-volume Burton with another commission – illustrations for Herman Melville's story *Benito Cereno* (1926). This time the illustrations were in colour – in fact, in real water-colour. A line drawing provided the key for each of the nine illustrations. Two colours were then added through stencils. This was a new speciality at the Curwen Press, then presided over by two very distinguished typographers, Harold Curwen and Oliver Simon. This stencil or 'pochoir' process was popular in Paris in the early twenties and was very successfully transplanted to England by the Curwen Press. A team of girls were trained and the department flourished for six years. Kauffer's partnership with Curwen was one of the outstanding successes in book production between the wars. The historian of this relationship, Dr Desmond Flower, has written that Kauffer 'made enormous demands of the Curwen Press department and they were met triumphantly'. Flower singled out the frontispiece for *Benito Cereno* as 'one of the most brilliant designs he ever conceived; with the pen and two tints – grey and mauve – he built up a shimmering design of a ship becalmed at last light which has an intricate beauty of which the eye can never tire' (plate 35). The special style Kauffer created for the process stands quite outside his other work.

Three further commissions followed at once: a two-volume *Don Quixote* with 21 illustrations for the Nonesuch Press (1930); *Robinson Crusoe* with seven illustrations and a vignette for Etchells and Macdonald (1929); nine illustrations and a vignette for Arnold Bennett's story *Elsie and the Child* published by Cassell (1929). Dr Flower has described the swift evolution in Kauffer's use of the process. For *Robinson Crusoe* and *Elsie and the Child* gouache was used rather than water-colour: the illustrations are literally as fresh as paint. But Kauffer also began to experiment with his 'key'. Flower has explained:

Illustrations which are going to be reproduced by stencil are usually made up of a drawing in pen or pencil on to which the artist adds his colour to taste; the basic drawing is called the key because, in addition to its primary purpose as part of the design, it serves also as a guide to the skilled girl who is applying the colour through the stencils. But in *Robinson Crusoe* the black key is used as an extra colour. There are large parts of the design in which no black occurs at all, but there are still enough patches for the operative to set her stencils by them. Another innovation was the use of spots of colour to break up a solid area of another colour or to reduce the brilliance of a patch of white. . . . Either while he was working on *Robinson Crusoe* or immediately thereafter, Kauffer tackled *Elsie and the Child.* He now had complete confidence in the stencil department of the Curwen Press and felt that he could afford to let himself go. He dispensed – for the first time in book illustration – with a key altogether; in other words, the girl who had to do the stencilling started with a blank sheet of paper and had to key all her stencils to one corner of it.[26]

Elsie and the Child remains the triumph of this collaboration, which was also characterized by typography of the greatest distinction in the books designed by Francis Meynell and Oliver Simon. Bennett produced another story for illustration by Kauffer, *Venus Rising from the Sea* (Cassell, 1931). Kauffer discarded two sets of drawings – the second set had been passed at stencil stage – before deciding on a third and final set. In these there is a key once more but colour is applied completely independently of it. The series of books closes on this experimental note. As Dr Desmond Flower put it: 'two things had happened: the gifted girls who had superbly stencilled thousands of designs had got married, and the cold wind of the slump had begun to blow'.[27]

ILLUSTRATIONS TO T.S. ELIOT

Although they were both members of the Council of the Arts League of Service, the acquaintance of Kauffer and T.S. Eliot did not ripen until the late twenties. In 1927 Eliot's publishing house Faber and Gwyer (later Faber and Faber) inaugurated their series of 'Ariel Poems'. These were well-printed (Curwen Press again) little folders – each containing one poem, with a line or colour woodcut frontispiece, and a design on the cover. Kauffer provided the illustration and cover design for the first issue in the series, Eliot's 'The Journey of the Magi'. Other examples of Eliot's new work appeared in the series with Kauffer's illustrations – 'A Song for Simeon' (1928), 'Marina' (1930) and 'Triumphal March', a fragment from the uncompleted 'Coriolan', appeared in similar format in 1931. It is unlikely that Eliot had much relish for any illustrations of his work. He once wrote to Kauffer: 'Yours is the only kind of decoration I can endure.'[28] Kauffer provided designs which at least avoid the prosaic, and open rather than block avenues of interpretation.[29] Eliot's poetry impressed him deeply. After a reading by Eliot in the autumn of 1928 he wrote to the poet: 'Your work awakens in me memories beyond myself and before myself . . . I am conscious too that I belong to something that I can't find here.'[30]

When Kauffer wrote to congratulate Eliot on 'For Lancelot Andrewes' (1928) the author gracefully responded with 'You seem to be the first person to look inside the book!'[31] In the following year Kauffer wrote 'I count it a genuine personal loss not to see you more often', and inquired whether Eliot would be interested in attempting a special edition of 'The Waste Land': 'I would like to do it – not illustrated – for that would be impossible – but perhaps suggestions arising from some of its sources.'[32] Nothing came of this idea, and although they discussed sets and

A Song for Simeon 1928 Frontispiece

Marina 1930 Frontispiece

costumes for *Sweeney Agonistes* Eliot never finished the play. Kauffer's first illustration-idea for 'Marna' included, he wrote to Eliot, 'the words "give, sympathise, control" as you have them in the "Waste Land" and indeed is there not in these three words the whole of equilibrium? They and the "freeing of the waters" run in my thoughts constantly. My admiration for what you do is one of the important things in my life.'[33] (Understandably Eliot did not want the 'Waste Land' 'stamped upon' 'Marina', and Kauffer prepared a second design without the words).[34] Kauffer was present at a dinner party after which Eliot read 'Ash Wednesday' aloud and invited criticism (in the event, Eliot only took seriously the suggestions offered by Virginia Woolf).[35] On 24 April 1930 Kauffer wrote to Eliot: 'I count this day one for which I am grateful for I believe it is publishing day for "Ash Wednesday". I am moved by the power of these magnificent poems. And I thank you for an experience that will become an influence.'[36]

Kauffer, always a great giver of gifts, presented Eliot with copies of his books – of *Robinson Crusoe* Eliot wrote: 'I like the illustrations immensely, and some of them have a quality which reminds me of Chirico, and which reminds me that it is my duty to finish the play [*Sweeney Agonistes*], so that the world may have the benefit of your scenery for it.'[37] Of Kauffer's *Don Quixote* Eliot wrote: 'I should not have thought anything possible after Doré, but you have done it.'[38] There was a touching bond between the two men – Eliot was even taken for Kauffer's brother by successive hall porters at Kauffer's apartment building – which became a close friendship over the next two decades.[39]

Eliot later gave an interesting account of the reasons for his friend's success, 'for such success as his needs a concurrence of causes':

First, of course, his great gifts, and I am thinking not only of his powers as an artist, but of the gift of sympathy and understanding which made him a good illustrator. I am grateful for his illustrations to my own 'Ariel' poems. *Second*, he found enlightened patrons to commission him. But perhaps one reason why he found such patrons was his personality: he had the kind of personality that attracts nice people. I daresay its attraction was still wider than that. But I mean that he had something deeper than is ordinarily implied by the word 'charm'. I mean that Ted Kauffer was an exceptionally loveable man.[40]

INTERIOR DESIGN: RUGS AND A STUDY

Kauffer and Marion Dorn held a joint exhibition of rugs made to their designs at Arthur Tooth & Sons Gallery in January and February 1929. The collection was woven by the Royal Wilton Carpet Company. The rugs were intended to complement the change in taste: a preference for bare walls and plain furniture. Decoration, banned from the walls, re-asserted itself on the floor. Indeed the rugs could also serve as hangings. Kauffer explained the idea behind the designs in an article:

The modern window is definitely wide and horizontal in form. The modern rug should, therefore, by its pattern, suggest the horizontal (which is also the restful). . . . Another effort was made to keep the rugs *concentric* rather than *eccentric*. Our idea, in other words, was that the pattern should be self-contained. Many of the old designs were of the all-over type that was to be imagined as repeating itself infinitely and extending invisibly into space beyond the actual boundaries of the rug. We consider that pattern is much more restful and dignified when it is a definite decoration within a fixed area and has a distinct relation to the limits of the room.[41]

There are relationships between Kauffer's rugs and his colour schemes and geometrical patterns in his graphic work – favoured colours were chocolate brown, beige, royal blue, navy blue. Colours were used in 'flat' areas in circles and squares. There are also, as in the graphics, reversal patterns of light and dark/figure and ground. The rugs are exemplary of good materials used with a simplicity that displays their richness without becoming showy; the colours are chosen with Kauffer's habitual refinement (plate 39). A more sumptuous carpet was commissioned from Kauffer by his friend Madge Garland (now Lady Ashton), who was one of *Vogue*'s lively team of editors in the twenties. This 5 × 11 foot carpet has a pattern of leopard spots and rectangles on an off-white ground. Further colours completed the design – pale shades of blue, yellow and green, and no less than three shades of brown. The colours were chosen to harmonize with the Bruton Street flat designed by Madge Garland for herself in 1930. The interior was predominantly white and dark brown: white walls, bookshelves and curtains (the latter made of white surgical rubber); a dark brown carpet and divan relieved by natural silk cushions of pale yellow and blue. Also to be taken into consideration were a square-armed chair by John Duncan Miller and a table with a thick blue-green glass top designed by Ronald Duncan.[42]

'We are very glad about the success of the rugs', Arnold Bennett wrote to Kauffer on 14 March 1929.[43] As a result of his work on *Elsie and the Child*, the novelist had every confidence in Kauffer's abilities. He commissioned Kauffer and Marion Dorn to design a study for him in his flat in the newly constructed apartment building Chiltern Court, Baker Street, into which the Bennetts moved in the autumn of 1929. For a short time Kauffer and Marion Dorn also took a flat there. The scheme included walls painted in 'delicate shades of pale beige, silver grey, yellow and grey-brown', with Kauffer rugs on the floor, a great range of steel shelving, and some square-ish but comfortable-looking furniture by E.A. Brown (probably designed under Kauffer's supervision).[44] Unfortunately, although some of the furniture survives, there is no record of the overall scheme, which, although more colours were used than in most present-day interiors, would have been intended by Kauffer to be not only lively but fundamentally 'restful'. Bennett resisted Kauffer's desire to arm his desk with a battery of gadgets: 'I have suppressed the dash-board gadget at the left of the desk, for bells, clock, lights, etc., as I don't need it. The leading idea of my desk is that it should be an *expanse*.'[45]

Bennett seems to have observed Kauffer with much of his novelist's shrewdness. Twenty years later Kauffer recalled, in an interview, that Arnold Bennett had compared him to 'a bird, forever in flight, forever searching for a place to come to rest'.[46]

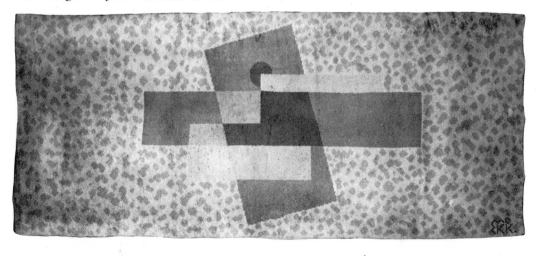

Rug designed for Madge Garland 1930

Portrait of Kauffer (early 30s) Photograph by Howard Coster

Chapter 5. **The Thirties (1)**

IN THE THIRTIES Kauffer became a very public figure in Britain, while remaining a very private man. The glimpses of him to be found in published recollections by friends and colleagues are few and precious. Remembrance imparted enchantment to Osbert Sitwell's passing reference to a boating trip 'on a golden Syracusan morning' with Kauffer, Marion Dorn and Adrian Stokes, 'in search of the Nymph Cyane in her fountain'.[1] We learn about his utter seriousness in professional matters, and in everything else, from some brief remarks by Dr Desmond Flower:

He was an aloof person not because he meant to be, but because so much of his time was spent in his private world. He took everything seriously, most of all himself. I had entered Cassells by the time *Venus Rising from the Sea* was in production, and it was over these illustrations that I first got to know him. His reason for tearing up a complete set of stencils already passed for press and beginning to work again at his own expense was that he did not think that he had quite caught what Bennett had in mind.[2]

Kauffer was fortunate in often finding clients who became close friends. In the thirties he struck up a new set of relationships in which professional and personal loyalties were intimately mixed. This gave him a valuable basis of trust between private and public worlds. The letters and recollections that have survived from the thirties allow a fuller picture of Kauffer's working methods, and himself, to come into view.

SWAN COURT

Kauffer and Marion Dorn moved into a newly built apartment block, Swan Court, Swan Walk, Chelsea, when the first tenancies became available in 1931. A range of studio flats on the eighth floor was a special feature of the building. They took Nos. 139 and 141, which had the advantage of a balcony running around two sides of what was a double flat. It was a smart, stimulating and expensive place to live. Their neighbours included the novelist L.H. Myers, Eliot's friend John Hayward, the American photographer and film-maker Francis Bruguière was just downstairs, the writer Bryan Guinness (now Lord Moyne) lived next door, and another close friend, Peter Gregory, was just across the passage. Kauffer's flat was always of impeccable orderliness. On the (then dashing) white linoleum and at the windows were Marion Dorn's rugs and curtains. The furniture was of natural wood finish and mostly built-in. There were important works of art: an African sculptured head, blown-up photographs by Man Ray, Jean Arp's painted relief *Constellation selon les lois du hasard* (now in the Tate Gallery), *Four Forms, drawings for sculpture* by Henry Moore (also now in the Tate), and one of the white painted reliefs of Ben Nicholson.[3] Kauffer was also the first man in England to buy a painting by the German experimental painter Willi Baumeister. This he bought from Freddie Mayor about 1930–32. Mayor used to lend Kauffer paintings from time to time – say a Klee water-colour which was beyond his means.[4] There were many books and the latest issues of magazines such as *Cahiers d'Art*.

Kauffer also had a collection of over 1000 gramophone records. These included many by Sibelius, of whose music he was very fond, but also 24 discs by Bing Crosby. A new friend of the early thirties, Kenneth Clark (now Lord Clark) who was then Director of the National Gallery, recalls the typical 'gadgetry' of Kauffer's studio: 'it was full of things that went up and down and in and out and had all the gadgetry of a surgery'.[5] Lord Clark regards the best description of Kauffer at this period as that written much later, in 1955, by Sir Colin Anderson:

Like a slim, russet eagle in appearance, and garbed in things which were at once slightly more *dégagés*, yet at the same time more elegantly combined than any garments one could have arranged upon one's own person, Ted Kauffer was a pleasure to the eye even without bringing into play his other pleasing characteristics. Cultured, intelligent and hypersensitive, his fastidiousness eternally governed his surroundings, his comings and goings, and his choice of company. One cannot remember anything he produced which hadn't the quality of orderliness and it was this, added to the brilliance of his basic conceptions, which made the impact of his work so dynamic. Neatness showed itself even in the arrangement of his work-bench and I well remember the astonishment of one of our children at the clinical order imposed upon it. His dazzling array of crayons, pens and pencils lay in regiments according to length (or so I seem to remember) so that one couldn't see how, having arranged them, he could bear to start work by breaking their ranks. . . . He was easy with children, like so many people who are less so with grown-ups.[6]

Kauffer was able to take on an assistant at this time, the young Sidney Garrad, who joined him direct from school. Sidney's first task every morning was to dust the studio from top to bottom – but the maid Betty had already dusted it once and Kauffer himself dusted it afterwards. Kauffer carried orderliness to an extreme, even laying out in sequence silk handkerchiefs, each in its separate cellophane, for each day of the week. Francis Bruguière, with the film-maker Oswell Blakeston as

Swan Court studio 1930s
Photographs by Kauffer

accomplice, once amused themselves by muddling them all up – to Kauffer's vexation. Lord Clark remembers Kauffer as 'the least Bohemian of men'.[7] Lady Mosley remembers Kauffer and Marion Dorn as 'Henry Jamesian Americans, the "innocent" sort James so often describes, who make Europeans appear to be devious. Whenever I gave a party [when she was married to Bryan Guinness] they always came and looked very tall and distinguished, and were I'm sure as good as gold. Although they were not married they were far more "respectable" than most of their London friends, and in a trivial way that was probably rather typical.'[8]

THIRTIES MODERNISM

In an article in the *Architectural Review* in November 1934 Wyndham Lewis gave an account of the success and failure of 'modernism' in England, and neatly places Kauffer's position in this development:

A very small number of 'highbrow' men and women meanwhile – a very small number – have supported these 'extreme' expressions of cubist, surréaliste, expressionist art. A handful of modernist villas have been run up; a few factories have gone cubist. Women's dress has been affected more than most things, but Victorian modes have always routed the 'robot' fashion, whenever it came to a stand-up fight. One shop in a hundred has acquired a chromium-plated modernist façade, but only in the very large cities. Yet one swallower of the new forms of expression does not make a summer – for the artist! And for one who was a swallower there have been a thousand who were non-swallowers – who with teeth set have violently rejected the medicine. For a *bitter pill* it is – why deny it? – this art of the most 'modern' schools. In this country architects like Etchells, Holden, Connell & Ward, Tecton, Emberton, Tait, Wells Coates, Chermayeff, McGrath, Fry, painters and sculptors like Henry Moore, Epstein, Kauffer and the Nashes are in the nature of paregoric or codliver oil to the over-sweet Anglo-Saxon palate; about that there is no question.

Like the passage from Evelyn Waugh's *Brideshead Revisited*, this quotation provides a useful context for Kauffer's work. 'Robot' fashion, for example, is a noticeable ingredient in the set of illustrations Kauffer

drew for a book published at the beginning of the new decade. This was Lord Birkenhead's *The World in 2030* published in 1930. Kauffer provided one illustration for each of the book's nine chapters of prognostication. He evidently used the air-brush to arrive at a cold, metallic surface for the robot figures of his science-fiction fantasies. A robot-like figure was invented by Kauffer for his major new patron of the thirties, Shell, and occurs in a more heraldic mood in the costumes he designed for the ballet *Checkmate* in 1937. Of the architects listed by Lewis, Etchells was a former X Group colleague of Kauffer's and commissioned the illustrations for *Robinson Crusoe*. Charles Holden achieved a lasting reputation for the Underground stations he designed for Pick in the thirties – and the Underground continued to be a major client for Kauffer.

Joseph Emberton's career as an architect offers parallels to that of Kauffer. Emberton designed fanciful exhibition pavilions in the early twenties that are not remote from Kauffer's style at the same period, he strikes a more emphatic geometric note on the façade of his Olympia building in 1929 – again, not distant from Kauffer at the same date – and reaches a much more assured International Style vocabulary in his Simpson's building in Piccadilly in 1936. Kauffer's work follows a similar evolution (and Simpson's came to him for designs at the same date).[9] Of the other architects, Chermayeff's designs for rugs are close to Kauffer's in style and Raymond McGrath won an *Architectural Review* competition for interior design in May 1930 with a scheme which included Kauffer rugs. Lewis was not overstating the case when he described what avant-garde artists were up against: Kauffer's daughter Ann visited Epstein's *Rima* monument to W.H. Hudson in Hyde Park

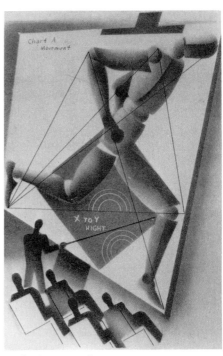

The Amenities of 2030 1930
Book illustration

with the sculptor's daughter, early in the thirties, only to find that Epstein's figure had been smeared with paint (presumably by a non-swallower of art of the most modern school).[10] Of the architects in Lewis's list the most remarkable was Wells Coates. He and Kauffer also worked together in the thirties and in a particularly interesting medium.

CRESTA, WELLS COATES AND THE PHOTO-MURAL

Cresta Silk was owned and directed by T.M. Heron, earlier an associate of Alec Walker – a client of Kauffer's Vorticist period. In 1930 Heron went to Kauffer for letter-headings, brand-labels and dress-boxes for his new firm. The letter-headings make excellent use of Eric Gill's newly available Sans Serif letter, use simple rules and circles as decoration and are embellished by a 'C S' monogram also designed by Kauffer. The same monogram, printed in chocolate brown on buff cardboard, was used for the dress-boxes in which the firm despatched its goods through the

Cresta letter-head 1929–30

Cresta dress box 1929–30

mails. Through an economical design requiring only one printing Kauffer gave the firm an abstract, witty and memorable trade-mark. The dresses themselves were distinguished – designers included the painters Paul Nash and Cedric Morris (and, in the forties, Heron's schoolboy son, Patrick). Perhaps even more important than these beautiful designs was the series of shop fronts which Cresta commissioned from Wells Coates. Coates's façade for Cresta's Bournemouth branch (1929)[11] has many of the qualities Stephen Tallents found in Mies van der Rohe's German pavilion in Barcelona in the same year. It might be claimed as the first modern shop front in England. The 'hygienic' shop had appeared in 1921 when MacFisheries transformed their premises in Old Bond Street, using only non-absorbent materials and eliminating mouldings.

By comparison with this, however, Coates's design is sublime. The company name became an integral part of his design: tall, elegant chrome letters, slim from the frontal plane but actually three-dimensional, receding grandly in depth to about 12 inches. The letters, and a series of circular light-fittings, are in carefully adjusted proportion to the main window – a wide oblong of plate-glass. The simplicity, spaciousness and elegance of this façade rebuke the bare, geometrical modernism of Emberton's Olympia building of the same year. Coates's position, at least by his own account, was not purely formalist – he described himself as less concerned with 'formal problems of style as with an *architectural* solution of the social and economic problems of today . . . the response that leads to freedom and fullness of life'.[12]

Pursuing this aim led Coates to enlist Kauffer's co-operation when he designed Embassy Court, on the sea-front at Brighton, in 1935. To establish a buoyant, cosmopolitan atmosphere for the building Kauffer was invited to design a mural in the entrance hall. Kauffer's design was an elaborate montage which combined photographic and painted elements – and the complete mural was in fact transferred to the walls by photographic means.[13] This was done by a process which had only recently been perfected by a firm of architectural decorators, Mollo and Egan. This firm was responsible for realizing Kauffer's Embassy Court photo-mural. First the wall was sprayed with photo-sensitive emulsion. Then, in dark-room conditions, the design was projected on to this. The

Embassy Court photo-mural 1935

image was developed, fixed and washed in situ. As in true fresco, image and wall are effectively one. The inventor of the process, Mr Eugene Mollo, experimented with different textured surfaces and once made a weird image by projecting a negative image of a sculpture back on to the sculpture itself. Needless to say, Kauffer was fascinated by the process. His design is a free assemblage – a sectional view of the Royal Pavilion, which stands half a mile down the road from Embassy Court, various Surrealist marine motifs (borrowed from the paintings of Edward Wadsworth), a baroque trumpeting angel in photo-montage with painted stars for musical notes, painted fishes and underwater plants, a nereid from the Étoile fountain in Paris (probably photographed by Kauffer himself, who was one of the first in England to acquire a Leica camera).

Kauffer wrote about the possibilities of the photo-mural at some length:

From my point of view this amazing invention is not revolutionary but a very natural extension of the camera as experience. Mural decoration, as we know, has come to a dead end both in subject matter and in surface texture. If the

Earl's Court photo-mural 1936

Earl's Court photo-mural 1936 Alternative design

Kauffer posters at Post Office Station 1930

heroic is desirable in decoration we can now project the documentary evidence to any scale required. Hardly any surface can resist photo-mural technique. Rippled, fluted, convex, concave, plaster, wood, metal, glass can be impregnated with this technique, applied so directly to the material that surface and picture become part of each other. Pictorial 'reporting' with the camera has now developed a wide interest in the various activities occurring in daily life. News reporting, scientific and microscopic photography, have revealed new and astonishing experience for the eye and imagination, and all the easy and quick registration that the camera can give should be used as part of modern decoration. It is the world we live in.

The designer should in no way be subordinated by the mass of material now under his eye. In fact, much more is now demanded of his talent; since it is for him to select and combine his material from a wide range of subject matter, surface textures, colour and colour treatment, exaggeration of scale, conflicts in pictorial interest dynamic and subtle, all depending upon the project. The range is wide, extending between the effects of splash headline dramatics to the quiet ease of a flight of birds or a classic head.

Surprise as an element in decoration is a factor which keeps the space alive, and in photo-mural technique the contrast between the painted line, pattern or symbol and the documentary photograph enlarged to fantastic scale and again designed for different materials, offers unlimited prospects to the imagination.

This medium now so ably handled by its inventors is the mural decoration of our time, and through this process we can extend our experience into new worlds of pleasure, surprise and wonder.[14]

Kauffer was not alone in taking to the new technique. With Francis Bruguière as photographer/designer Mollo and Egan made a giant photo-mural for the British Pavilion at the Paris Exhibition in 1937. They had decorated over 400 cinemas in Britain by the war, which brought the process to an end. (Mollo moved on to new interests after the war.) Kauffer employed the process again in 1936 as the main feature of an exhibition about 'London's New Entertainment Centre', Earl's Court. Pick had begun to use part of the Charing Cross Underground station as an exhibition hall. Here the model for the Earl's Court building was shown. Behind it was a huge photo-mural by Kauffer. The ubiquitous and industrious Kauffer was already involved with the new building, as designer of an emblematic knight in armour which still decorates its east façade. Pick also commissioned him to design posters and car-cards publicizing the new exhibition centre. The photo-mural uses 'splash headline dramatics', counterpointed by an abstract space-frame. Splendid divers float like birds, giant ice-hockey players jostle, street-crowds mill, within an elastic framework of lines and colours. Kauffer got the building off to a good start.[15]

FRIENDS AND ASSOCIATES: PETER GREGORY AND LUND HUMPHRIES

Peter Gregory lived opposite Kauffer in Swan Court and their flats offered a rich contrast in style. Gregory's was all untidy confusion, overflowing with books and pictures; Kauffer's was grand and immaculate. And yet Gregory was in a sense Kauffer's patron. Eric Craven Gregory (1887–1959), Peter among his friends, was one of two sheet-anchors for Kauffer's career in the thirties (the other, Jack Beddington of Shell, will be described in the next chapter). Sir Philip Hendy described Gregory as 'a handsome embodiment of the bluff and kindly Yorkshireman of fiction'.[16] Another friend, Sir Herbert Read, said that Peter Gregory was 'a man of perfect natural goodness'.[17] He was a tall, bear-like man whose kindliness was blended with shrewdness – 'an intuition for the balance sheet' – from which organizations with which

Peter Gregory 1930
Photograph by Kauffer

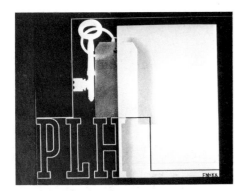

Lund Humphries change of
address card 1932

he concerned himself, from the *Burlington Magazine* to the Institute of Contemporary Arts (and including several struggling art schools). were handsome beneficiaries. Hendy went so far as to say (writing in 1959) 'Peter Gregory perhaps played a larger part in the art history of the past forty years than any man who was not an artist'. Although his name is remembered in the generous endowments he left for artists and poets, such achievements as his are often lost to view.

Gregory became a director of the Bradford printing firm Percy, Lund, Humphries in 1919. He knew Kauffer from 1919 or 1920. The firm published a set of artist's Christmas cards in 1920 and one of these was illustrated by Kauffer. Gregory became a joint managing director of the firm in 1930 with Eric Humphries. Humphries was a master printer whose expertise was called upon in 1939–40 during an early stage in the development of atomic power. His outstanding knowledge of engraving techniques put him in a position to advise on the possibilities of making an ultra-fine copper membrane. Humphries ran the Bradford works, while Gregory controlled the business end in London. Kauffer's close association with the firm during the thirties began when Lund Humphries moved their offices from Amen Corner to 12 Bedford Square in 1932. Kauffer designed the change of address card, using a technique related to Man Ray's 'Rayographs' – burned-out whites and solid blacks. The Bedford Square building had enough space for an exhibition gallery to be constructed on the ground floor. This was designed by the architects Hall, Easton and Robertson, with a specially designed floor by Marion Dorn – who also contributed one of her finest hand-woven rugs – and opened in December 1933.[18]

The first exhibition was shared by Kauffer with Francis Bruguière. Artist and photographer also worked together on schemes for Charnaux, makers of patent latex corsets. Bruguière photographed models standing in front of nude figures drawn by Kauffer. They also worked with a paper-model maker called Dronsfield on projects advertising Spey Royal whisky (Kauffer again providing the background illustrations).[19] Lund Humphries gave Man Ray his first London exhibition in the following year – which drew the august presence of Marcel Duchamp to Bloomsbury. A dark-room had been set up at 12 Bedford Square, as well as a studio for Kauffer, and Man Ray used both in 1935. It was probably through Kauffer that Man Ray's experimental films were shown in London (at the Film Society), and he

Studio at Lund Humphries 1930s

AS YOU LOOK through these pages you will find that we have
set out to tell you fairly what Charnaux Belts can do, to show you
by photographs, striking in their accuracy and simplicity, exactly
what they are.

Charnaux Belts are created from electrically deposited Latex, a
new material with unrivalled capacity for stretch and returning to
shape; they can be washed and dried in a few minutes; they are
cool, light and exquisite to wear. The Latex has thousands of
perforations graduated in size and scientifically arranged to produce bands of force. These bands of force are designed to give
not only upward support to the figure but also freedom of movement; they incite the abdominal muscles to do their normal work
more efficiently and by promoting their activity reduce fatigue.
The thousands of perforations obviously allow the skin to trans-
pire unimpeded.

Charnaux Belts are beautiful in themselves; they will add to the
beauty of your figure, and they will give you the attraction of an
'uncorsetted' look and the smooth lines which
have made Charnaux enthusiasts of so many dress
designers.

Charnaux brochure 1935
Photograph by Man Ray, layout by Kauffer

was certainly responsible for the introductions which resulted in Man
Ray's portraits of T.S. Eliot, Virginia Woolf and Aldous Huxley. It seems
likely that Kauffer also got the Underground to commission a pair of
posters from Man Ray – a mysterious set which eventually appeared in
1939. One collaboration between the two is known – again a brochure
for Charnaux, which has a Man Ray photograph of a Venus de Milo cast
and layout by Kauffer.

Man Ray recalled that Kauffer was a regular visitor to Paris in the
thirties, that he seemed restless and driven, and that on these visits he
experimented with opium – not a rare or unknown quantity in Paris in
artistic circles at the time.[20] Man Ray photographed Kauffer, probably in
1936, and his portrait brings out the aquiline quality noticed by Sir
Colin Anderson – it is a crystalline, aristocratic, Cocteau-like head. (No
reproducible print survives and the negative is lost.)[21] Bruguière also

made a portrait of Kauffer – this time a more intimate and relaxed study. A third portrait was made by the London studio photographer and portrait specialist, Howard Coster. In this Kauffer seems to be entirely in his private world; the delicacy of the lighting and subtlety of the facial modelling recall a remark from Madge Garland, that Kauffer was 'a man born without a skin'.

Another important exhibition at Lund Humphries was shown in 1935 – the first in England of the great typographical innovator Jan Tschichold. It is hard to assess the influence of these exhibitions but it is at least likely that this one prepared the ground for Tschichold's post-war appointment at Penguin Books – which broadcast his standards very widely indeed. Kauffer also introduced the immigrant German graphic designer Hans Schleger, professionally known as Zero, to English design circles with an exhibition in 1934. This skilled designer made many contributions to the visual environment in Britain – from London bus stop signs to trade-marks for MacFisheries and the John Lewis Partnership, colophons for Allen Lane and Penguin Educational Books, and a whole series of distinguished Edinburgh Festival posters – including the familiar castle and dove motif. Perhaps some credit for this string of achievements goes to the exhibition with which an emigré from Nazi Germany, struggling to adapt to a new country, was set on his feet.

The gallery also introduced the poster partnership of Lewitt-Him, described by Kauffer in the catalogue in these terms: 'They are comic, they are amusing, they are thoughtful, they are serious, and they are good advertising.' They were, in fact, just the designers for the home-front campaigns of the Second World War, when they made their most important contribution. *Eight Commercial Artists* were shown in 1934 which included two of Kauffer's growing number of imitator-disciples, Peter Morgan and Theyer Lee-Elliott.

In the same year the gallery showed the first seven years' production of the Cresset Press. The Press was founded by Dennis Cohen in 1927 and began with typical private press luxury items such as an edition of *The Shepheard's Calendar*, printed by George W. Jones ('At the Sign of the Dolphin') – a now obscure typographer, but one much admired by Tschichold. Cohen soon became an arch-Modernist, notably as the man who commissioned houses from both Mendelsohn and Chermayeff and Gropius and Fry, which stand side by side in Old Church Street, a stone's throw from Swan Court. Cresset Press moved into the contemporary field with illustrations by Edward Burra, D.H. Lawrence's *Birds, Beasts and Flowers*, the English edition of *Tobacco Road* and H.G. Wells's *Things to Come*, for which Kauffer provided the jacket in 1935. Kauffer's jacket draws on Sir Alexander Korda's film version of Wells's futuristic text, *The Shape of Things to Come*. In the twenties Kauffer had often used new type-faces produced by the Klingspor type-foundry in Germany, notably the Narcissus and Neuland display faces. Lund Humphries staged an exhibition of the foundry's work.

Kauffer himself showed a full range of his work at the gallery in 1935. It was widely reviewed. For the *Scotsman* Kauffer was 'the Picasso of advertising design'. The *Guardian* found a very different likeness: 'His strict and exciting personality has entered into the accepted life of our time as sharply as Noel Coward has through the bias of his characters and songs.'[22] D.S. MacColl, however ('The Iniquity of Fashion', *London Mercury*, May 1935) complained that Kauffer had been 'too easily contented by his flatterers and his own readiness, and has missed the difficult track'. MacColl, who did not like Cézanne either, did not say

Things to Come 1935 Book jacket

where that track might lie and was perhaps guilty of mere spleen.

The most thoughtful and perceptive review came from a young art historian called Anthony Blunt (later Professor Sir Anthony Blunt, Surveyor of the Queen's Pictures and Director of the Courtauld Institute of Art). Blunt's review provides the best account of Kauffer's standing at mid-decade. His words also make a companion-piece to Roger Fry's assessment in the mid-twenties. The whole article is reprinted here:

Mr McKnight Kauffer is an artist who makes me resent the division of the arts into major and minor. Since he is not a pure painter or sculptor or architect, but an illustrator and a designer of book-covers and posters, he must, technically, be classed as minor, but as I looked round the exhibition of his work at Messrs Lund Humphries's galleries in Bedford Square I was led to think: 'If he is minor, who then is major – at any rate among his English contemporaries?' For Mr Kauffer does to perfection everything to which he sets his hand, and it is only our inherited prejudice that somehow a poster is always a frivolity that prevents us from fully acknowledging his brilliance.

I hope that Mr Kauffer will not take offence if I suggest that his achievement is really parallel with that of a very good translator of literature. (He will, I think, forgive me if he recollects that this puts him aesthetically parallel with the Anglican divines who composed the Authorized Version of the Bible.) He has not himself invented any of the important styles such as Cubism or Superrealism which have appeared in the last thirty years, nor has he even taken a direct part in their inception. What he has done is rather to take from these styles as soon as they appeared exactly those elements which were relevant to his particular purposes and has translated these elements into terms of illustration or poster art. It is remarkable how quick off the mark Mr Kauffer has always been. In 1919 he was using the methods of the later kinds of Cubism, and by 1926 he had already spotted the possibilities of Superrealism and used its methods in a poster of the British Museum representing a large statue of Socrates. Superrealism, with its direct reliance on appeal to the sub-conscious, ought to be the art perfectly adapted to the poster, and Mr Kauffer has fully exploited it. His adaptation of the deliberate distortion of perspective practised by the Superrealists and his play with certain repeated motifs, such as the raised hand, all produce posters which arrest and slightly puzzle the passer-by. But, apart from producing admirable posters, Mr Kauffer has rendered another important service to modern art. By using the methods of the more advanced schools and by putting them before the men in the street in such a way as to catch them off their guard, so that they are lured into liking the poster before they realize that it is just the kind of thing which they loathe in the exhibition gallery, by this means he has familiarized a very wide public with the conventions of modern painting and has greatly increased the chances which modern painters, who are not involved in publicity, have of being appreciated and widely enjoyed.[23]

The last idea in Blunt's review was also expressed, in a characteristically neat turn of phrase, by T.S. Eliot: 'He did something for modern art with the public as well as doing something for the public with modern art.'[24] Lord Clark regards Blunt's comparison of Kauffer to a good translator as the most apt definition of his talent, and suggests that it was 'mediumistic, something that came up from inside him'.[25] His free use of available styles is probably not unconnected with his generosity to other artists, which Gregory described as 'a totally unselfish respect for style in others'.[25]

MARION DORN LTD

Marion Dorn founded her own company in 1934. Her output is so extensive and distinguished that it needs a separate study,[27] but the recollections of her assistant in the thirties, Elizabeth Edwards (now Lady Robinson), afford a glimpse of her show-room and studio which should be recorded.[28] Her premises were at 10 Lancashire Court, off Bond Street, and were one of the exciting places to visit in thirties

Marion Dorn 1930s
Upside-down portrait by Kauffer

London. A stable was converted into a ground-floor stock-room and office, while the upper floor was show-room and studio combined. The upper floor was white and airy, 'communicating a sense of quality and detail, a Bauhaus feeling', Lady Robinson remembers. Lengths of fabric were thrown through chromium rings attached high up on the wall – now a standard display method. Marion Dorn collected objects which exhibited colours or textures she liked – so there would be neatly laid out pieces of emerald bottle glass, reels of bright copper wire.

Work in progress was indicated by a drawing-board, poster colours in pots, renderings of different colourways of a design being carried out as time allowed. She had a strong preference for sparkling white as a ground for bright patterns derived from floral forms. For upholstery she liked hand-woven Welsh tweeds in shades of green; for curtains, yellow – especially in small rooms. Sometimes she used very expensive materials – for example, curtains figured with vines and grapes for a

Cambridge Combinations Room ran to £6 a yard. On the other hand she showed that simple materials could be used with distinction – for example a pair of screen curtains for the Paris Cinema: terracotta hessian with two enormous stripes of white cotton rag at the meeting edges. Clearly Kauffer and Dorn's relationship included shared professional opportunities – among these was the work they did for the Orient Line, flagship of the interior design of modern ocean liners.

THE ORIENT LINE

Ocean liners became part of the scrapbook of functionalist design for young architects in the twenties and thirties, along with grain elevators and even tobacco pipes. The sweeping lines and no-nonsense engineering of the superstructure of these modernist paragons tended, on the other hand, to house Scottish baronial ballrooms and other schizophrenic aberrations. Colin Anderson decided to cure this by building an integrated ocean liner – the *Orion* (1935). The architect Brian O'Rorke was given the overall commission for the interior design. Sir Colin Anderson later wrote of this radical revision:

Orient Line symbol 1935–7

The sheer struggle represented by the creation of the *Orion* was immense, for almost all the components that made up her appearance had to be specially designed and made for her. For instance, we were setting out to escape not only from the shape of every handle but from the dominance of brass as a material. We were a spearhead of the use of white metal at sea, though aluminium was not itself yet freely available and anodyzing was a new word. We were fighting the baroque figuration of veneered panelling and insisting that straight and uneventful grain was what we must have. We were rejecting all the damask patterns, all the floral patterns, the cut velvet, plush and chintz, the 'galon', the bobbles and the vaguely Louis cutlery.[29]

What Anderson and O'Rorke were after was not actually on the market, and they found some difficulty in 'persuading proud and successful industries that not a single object in their entire output was acceptable for a modern ship interior'. Anderson makes the significant remark that these firms had no staff designers who understood what was wanted, and 'there were no such people as industrial designers. There were a few artist designers, if one knew where to look for them.' Anderson, who had Tommy Tallents (brother of Stephen) on his board of directors, knew where to look. Among the artist designers involved in the *Orion*, Kauffer gave general advice and encouragement, draughtsmanship, design know-how and typographic advice. Marion Dorn designed her first 'sea-going' rugs. They also contributed to the sister-ship *Orcades* (1937). Kauffer designed posters for the Orient Line, invitations and brochures for the new ships, and for the *Orion* he designed an engraved glass mirror.[30] At 9 × 13 feet this must have been impressive. Kauffer's design showed Orion the Giant in constellation form. The mirror was ripped out when the ship was converted for war use.

Orient Line labels 1935

Kauffer also designed some of the minutiae of ocean travel – luggage labels. There are tie-on ones in stylish combinations such as raspberry and pink or lime and black, and there is a set of circular adhesive ones. These belong to a different era from his bright little pictures for Steinthal & Co. They fulfil the Functionalist aesthetic of the line. Kauffer divided the label into two halves, printed the lower half black with the words Orient Line 'reversed-out'. The upper half is also divided, the right side printed in primary red, the left printed with the letter which designated the part of the ship for which the luggage was destined. The alphabet

was a slab-serifed Rockwell face, which Kauffer liked to use at this period like slabs of paint. It is a satisfyingly balanced and immediately recognizable design. A formal ambiguity of pattern occurs with some letters, surely intentionally (considering Kauffer's Cresta monogram) – for example in the confronted arrow-head shapes in the 'X' label. This minute little visual nuance is worth mentioning only because it is characteristic of Kauffer's interest in the last detail of any design.

INSTITUTIONALIZATION OF INDUSTRIAL ART

Aubrey Beardsley once wittily remarked that the poster artist was 'déclassé – on the street'. For Ashley Havinden and others, part of Kauffer's importance was as a leader of a new profession: 'Before his time, most people working in advertising design were disappointed "fine" artists. Kauffer, through his posters, helped to establish the career of designing for advertising as a worthwhile vocation.' The Society of Industrial Artists was founded in 1930: Kauffer served on its Council and was one of the first Honorary Fellows appointed. Frank Pick chaired the Council for Art and Industry set up in 1934 and brought in Kauffer as a Council member. In 1935 Kauffer joined the Advisory Council of the Victoria and Albert Museum. In 1936 he became the first Honorary Designer for Industry, a faculty of 40 (now 60) chosen by the Royal Society of Arts. This title was intended to provide designers with professional recognition comparable to the Royal Academicians. The faculty soon received permission to add Royal to the title. In the late thirties Kauffer often signed his posters Hon. RDI. (The honorary nature of the award in Kauffer's case was because he was not a British subject.)

The Design and Industries Association, founded in 1915, of which Kauffer was an early member, had prepared the ground for these developments but had soon run out of steam. In 1936 Kauffer explained why the D.I.A. was unsuccessful: 'It has been very gentlemanly in its habits, it has had too much good taste and it has concentrated on the hand-made rather than the machine made.'[31] Welcoming a new magazine in that year, Kauffer wrote to its editors:

If your magazine really intends to find out why industrial design is on the whole so characterless in England then your research will have to begin with the art teaching now going on in the various schools, with the buyers in the multiple shops and then with the manufacturers and finally with the public.[32]

This was very much the approach adopted by the young emigré design historian, Nikolaus Pevsner, whose book *An Inquiry into Industrial Art in England* was published in the following year.

With the Empire Marketing Board government had acknowledged the role of designers. When Stephen Tallents left the E.M.B. to become first Public Relations Officer at the General Post Office, he promised former colleagues at a farewell dinner that he was going to 'sing the E.M.B.'s song in a strange land'.[33] Tallents took the Film Unit with him and another masterpiece of documentary resulted in 1936, *Night Mail* (embellished by the Auden poem and Benjamin Britten's music). For Tallents Kauffer designed posters, publicity cards, and an exhibition stand. Institutional agencies in publicity developed in pace with the new profession of industrial designers.

Typical of the many design initiatives of the decade was a large exhibition of modern British industrial art arranged by the Royal Society of Arts at the Royal Academy in 1935. The exhibition had this lofty intention: 'To encourage British artists to give to industry the

Come on the Telephone 1934 Brochure

benefit of their talent and training, so that the objects with which we are surrounded in our daily lives may have an appearance which is not only attractive, but is based on genuinely artistic principles.' Herbert Read condemned the exhibition as mere 'novelism' – neither functional nor specifically modern. In particular the poster section was 'an outrageous misrepresentation of what is actually being done by artists in this country'.[34] Kauffer was not represented in the section; when Read inquired why he was told that Kauffer had been excluded because he was not British. 'Nothing' Read concluded, 'could so openly reveal the abject futility of the exhibition.' The Royal Society of Arts made amends with its award to Kauffer the following year. The episode does underline, however, that official initiatives were of far less consequence for designers like Kauffer than the patronage of clients in the commercial sector. One of the most important of these, Jack Beddington of Shell-Mex B.P. Ltd, forms much of the subject of the next chapter.

Portrait of Kauffer 1930s Photograph by Francis Bruguière

Chapter 6. **The Thirties (2)**

PETER GREGORY was one sheet-anchor for Kauffer in the thirties, Jack Beddington was another. Jack Beddington (1893–1959) was a son of one of seven brothers called Cohen who were all members of the London Stock Exchange in the 1890s. The brothers collectively and simultaneously changed their name to Beddington (the name of a Surrey village). A story is told of the newly named brothers arriving for work one morning to find emblazoned across the main hall of the Stock Exchange 'And the Lord said unto Moses – Good Morning Mr Beddington!' Jack Beddington read Classical Moderations at Oxford and, like Tallents, survived the First World War only by being almost killed in it. He was severely wounded at Ypres in 1915 and invalided home. After the war he joined Shell and was posted to China for eight years. A short spell in the Oxford office was followed by his appointment as Publicity Manager in 1928 or 1929. In 1932 Shell and British Petroleum decided to combine their publicity and trading operations in the United Kingdom by setting up a separate company – Shell-Mex B.P. Ltd. Beddington became director responsible for publicity in the new company, answerable only to the General Manager, W. Halford.

Beddington made the most of his new opportunities. Lord Clark remembers him as looking like 'an amiable Levantine pirate'.[1] Professor Richard Guyatt has described him as 'a wizard, albeit a suave and worldly wizard'.[2] Beddington was fond of quoting Wilde's remark 'Enough is never as good as a feast.' He was a warm, buoyant and practical man. On taking over publicity he did one seemingly trivial, but typical, thing. He arranged for designers' fees to be paid directly from his own department. In this way payments did not have to be churned through an elaborate and lengthy accounting procedure which dealt in very large sums of money. Designers were paid as soon as final art-work was approved. Beddington knew what the Design and Industries Association was doing but Pick's concrete example impressed him more. He also recognized the possibilities of film and recruited two of Grierson's young directors, Stuart Legg and Arthur Elton. In 1932 he sponsored Paul Rotha's first film, *Contact*. He brought in promising literary men like Peter Quennell and John Betjeman, the illustrator Nicholas Bentley, established a studio under Tom Gentleman, and hired the photographer Maurice Beck. Betjeman began the lively and idiosyncratic series of Shell County Guides, a celebrated series which included Paul Nash's Dorset volume (and inspired Nash to a set of fine photographs).

Beddington had a serious interest in the art of his own time. He was a nephew of Sidney and Violet Schiff, who were among the very few who had commissioned work from the short-lived sculptor Henri Gaudier-Brzeska. Six de Chirico paintings hung in their drawing-room in Ilchester Place. Beddington's cousin Sir Edward Beddington-Behrens commissioned Stanley Spencer's Burghclere murals and maintained Oskar Kokoschka during the Second World War. Bryan Robertson has described Beddington as 'a man who really understood artists and continually sought new means of patronage without ever becoming patronizing in his own manner' – which was, Robertson added, 'unfailingly warm-hearted and full of fun'.[3] His collection included many works by artists who are not famous or even well-known – a sure sign of collecting for the love not the prestige of art – and he bought from artists who genuinely needed support. On occasion he bought paintings which he thought the artist might have difficulty in selling elsewhere. He was a familiar figure, rushing out at lunchtimes to see new shows and follow up artists who interested him. His collection included works by Wyndham Lewis, Sickert, David Bomberg, Merlyn Evans, L.S. Lowry and Bernard Cohen – also two water-colours by Kauffer, who resumed painting in 1931.[4]

Shows of Kauffer's water-colours and gouaches were held at Tooth's in 1931 and 1933. A stay at Clive Bell's villa behind Cassis in the South of France resulted in enough work for the 1931 show (which included original designs for book illustrations) and a second trip produced the landscapes shown at Tooth's in 1933. Some individual works are far above 'holiday painting' and achieve real distinction: suitably 'poster-ized', the style of his paintings appears in a landscape series of posters for the Great Western Railway published in 1932. The Beddingtons acquired a Kauffer rug for the house in Lansdowne Road which they took in June 1929. It is one of Kauffer's most successful rugs, in navy blue, black, off-white and beige.[5]

Later in the same year Kauffer wrote to Beddington and his wife Olivia to thank them for offering him a stay in the country. Kauffer says that he has too much work on but hopes to get over to Paris soon:

This will be a change for me – which is all that I need. And it will be a stimulus as well – also all I need – for Paris thrills me with its constant surprises, its continual surprises, its continual experiment – all the painting – all the designing – all the new ideas.[6]

On this visit he felt the influence of his great French counterpart,

'A Plain Publicity Manager':
Jack Beddington 1930s
Drawing by Rex Whistler

Medical aid to Spain poster (about 1936)

A.M. Cassandre. Kauffer's 16-sheet poster for *Pratt's High Test Motor Spirit* (of which a copy was given to the Victoria and Albert Museum in 1931, presumptively the date of its use) has dramatically receding telegraph poles which are derived from Cassandre's *La Route Bleue* of 1929.[7]

Kauffer's relations with Pick were those of an enthusiastic professional who liked to discuss art with his client. With Beddington the relationship was social, and they and Olivia and Marion were often together at the Café Royal, the Gargoyle Club, the Ivy Restaurant or the Savoy Grill. Kauffer's letters to Beddington are the only surviving clues to his inner life at this period. They are often uninformative in themselves but are worth recording as evidence of the kind is so rare. Without such letters Kauffer might seem a mere designing machine. Kauffer wrote to Beddington – away on a business trip to America in 1935 – of the excitement of having his posters on the streets. 'My new posters have all been printed now and I am longing to see them up.' He goes on:

I have kept so close to my studio that I've seen no one. Man Ray is over – sends his best to you. Eric [Gregory?] has gone to Spain until Boxing Day. I've not seen Grierson or Philip [?]. I'm doing some new Underground things – there is a great wave of pro-Chinese ideas – and the weather is sad – and I wonder often and often what it is all about! I would like to do great things with my designing – but I never seem to get there. I wish you were here – I need to talk to you.[8]

In 1936 Kauffer and Marion separated temporarily with the aim of discovering each other afresh. Kauffer went alone to Aix-en-Provence in May on a painting expedition and wrote back to the Beddingtons. Writing on the notepaper of the Café des Deux Garçons he explained that 'the name of this café does not signify that I have changed my morals':

I am starting to paint in dead earnest. Up to now I have with weather permitting made attempts – but the results have been discouraging. Hoping and working towards being a good artist requires courage – for when one sees how miserable results can be – to face the problem again and again and still with failure – does I say require a courage which most people do not understand. I wish I could stay on until about August. I could I feel get a really good show for the autumn. . . . I like the quiet life I lead here. I am early to bed – and up early in the morning. I see Matthew Smith at least once a day and we have become quite intimate friends. He is very interesting and has the greatest of charm. He and I are in very similar situations oddly enough. Our conversation however is not confined to our problem. I think he is England's finest painter as perhaps you know. . . .[9]

It is interesting that Kauffer should have preferred the sensuous, even luscious, work of the painterly Smith over the austere abstractions of Ben Nicholson or the Surrealism of Wadsworth (although Francis Bacon shared the preference). Of the trio, Smith represented the most traditional kind of painting in his exuberant renditions of nudes, landscapes and still-life. Kauffer wrote again a week or two later:

Matthew Smith has gone now and I find that I had grown very fond of him – because I miss him. Vague and never knowing what he is going to do next – full of anxieties – nervous – shy – yet so very charming. He wrote me a note when he left – began 'cher ami' and there is something touching about this. . . .

I get bored to death with a man by name E.McK.K. so much so that I could easily kill the b-----d (ask Jack). I have done two watercolours that I am willing to take my hat off to and when the rain stops again I feel I am now on the track of big business. Jack – you must not worry about my gambling – playing with

Aldous Huxley's Garden, Provence
(about 1932) Gouache

francs does not amuse me and since I can play with no higher stakes – I don't play because I don't wish to be bored with petty winnings or petty losses. So the old paternal spirit can park its hips!

... A young Scotsman whom I did not meet stayed here two days – told the proprietor I was a big shot in England and the proprietor came rushing up to me so out of breath that I thought the place had caught on fire – but just to say 'I now know who you are' to which I replied 'Achille, you're telling tales out of school.' He is a funny little man and I have always joked with him and by doing this kept getting my pension cheaper. But he had the first laugh on me because I tried to tell him when I first arrived that I was an artist – But what I evidently said was 'I am a painting' – sounds pretty conceited to me.[10]

Kauffer also wrote to Beddington when both were in England, sometimes asking for payment at the 'rough' stage of a design. On 1 April 1937 he wrote:

You are always so sympathetic and good to me – I hesitate to ask any special consideration – but I thought the Aeroplane job would be well complete by now and I promised to pay my income tax on Monday. I have other things finished for which payment is due – but these are not yet turning up! I have been passing through a strange – slow period which always precedes a new development in my work – but which is painful and often very impractical. As I get older these periods become more insistent – I suppose the years behind and the years coming wedge one in between – experience past and hope for the future. My domestic life is completely happy – and Marion's sweet devotion strengthens me – but there is this persistent desire to go further and further with my work – which if I allowed to take possession of me would be disastrous from an economic standpoint. This is my problem, my *mal de coeur* – only this.

Kauffer's phrase the 'Aeroplane job' might give rise to speculation, given his status as a design all-rounder. In fact he did design the exterior colour scheme, or livery, of an aeroplane. This was the Handy-Heck plane developed for Whitney Straight in 1932–3. Only one was produced. A water-colour records Kauffer's stylish livery for it in chocolate brown and black.[11] He also designed other items for Straight's Aluminum Ltd, such as desk sets which were apparently used at

Aeroplane livery 1932–3
Water-colour by Crichton Nuthall

Shell Lorry 1930s

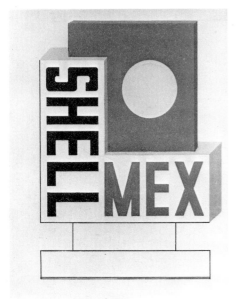

Design for petrol pump top 1934

Lubrication by Shell 1937 Poster

Claridge's and the Savoy Hotel. The 1937 job was probably an 'Aero-Shell' poster incorporating a photograph of the Miles-Whitney Straight aeroplane. The poster uses the 'space-frame' device which Kauffer tried out in his photo-mural for the Earl's Court exhibition at Charing Cross Station, a simple spatial illusion in which the aeroplane takes off. The device is of great consequence for Kauffer's last and finest work in the theatre, in this same year, which will be discussed below.

The poster was one of a whole series of 'lorry bills' Kauffer designed for Shell in the thirties. The series ranks as one of Kauffer's more grand achievements. The bills were printed to a size of 30 × 45 inches. Beddington had seen to it in 1929, when he first began his publicity work, that Shell advertising was disciplined.[12] Instead of disfiguring rural areas, posters were shown on the sides of the company's lorries. The lorries were painted green and red and even in the early thirties the drivers sat up exposed to the weather in cabs without windscreens. In the back was a large tank and a set of oil-drums kept in by cattle-truck sides. On each side and across the tailboard were special panels for the bills, which framed them with a trim black margin. This was how Kauffer's Shell posters were usually seen in the 1930s, although some of the lorry bills were also printed at '48 sheet' size, 10 × 20 feet. An example is the 1933 B.P. Ethyl poster (see plate 42), which is altered when one imagines it at the size of a hoarding: so too is one's appreciation of the audacity of Beddington's campaign. He was a bold client but perhaps not as advanced in taste as his principal designer. Kauffer designed an extraordinarily advanced petrol pump top for Shell-Mex in 1934 – a simple but revolutionary abstract design in primary red and yellow, which was never used.

The letter to Beddington suggests an anxious period of preparation for change. A few months later Kauffer designed a poster which embodies this change. It is the one poster which Kauffer described his working methods for, and it is an account reinforced in interest by some recollections from his assistant Sidney Garrad.

NEW SHELL LUBRICATING OILS 1937 (Plate 41)

The starting-point is a discussion with the client (Beddington) which releases a swarm of first impressions of the product – and some internal questions like 'Will my client understand what I propose to do? Will he trust an intuitive solution to the problem?'[13] Back in his studio Kauffer settles down to experiment with different weights of lettering, different ways of presenting the actual product – a conical oil-can, with a red robot symbol on it (based on an artist's lay-figure) which Kauffer had designed some years earlier. He looks for some way of balancing lettering and product, and reaches a point where the two ingredients establish 'a direction which seems to suit the character of the product. If this is so a new *stimulus* is set up.' At this point he remembers that when the client gave him the name of the product 'a ribbon came into my mind'. 'Now why did I associate the movement of a ribbon with the product at the time of our interview? A ribbon, so I think, suggests smoothness, softness – yes. . . . I accept the ribbon as a symbol – so now I have three parts to my design. The framework, as it were, is complete.' With relief he can now put the client out of his mind. What about the public? is his next consideration. A suggestion of speed is discounted – 'only a few specialists are allowed this extravagance'. But 'the design nevertheless should express movement – smooth curvilinear move-ment – a suggestion that everything is working well.' He devises a scheme to convey this idea. A contrast between an oily black ground, purple ribbon, yellow lettering and red and yellow oil-can establish an attention-getting colour scheme. The ribbon provides the co-ordinating link and implies the reading order of the words.

Kauffer went on to speak of the 'latent symbolism' of his ribbon. The poster was intended to satisfy client, public and also himself. The ribbon, in a sense, represents 'Kauffer-as-Artist'. He thought it was related to an act of spontaneous, intensified vision when 'a strip of cardboard fell from one of my shirts as I took it out of a drawer. I started to pick it up off the floor and suddenly became aware of something unusual in the shapes of light and dark.' The fascination was genuine, if inexplicable, and he began to draw the card from different angles. Sidney Garrad remembers that the poster was designed during another bout of separation from Marion Dorn. Kauffer took a room at the Mount Royal Hotel in Oxford Street. He repeatedly drew lengths of ribbon – throwing actual pieces over his shoulder and then drawing them in poster colours as they lay. As was often the case Sidney was entrusted with the task of enlarging the design for lithographic printing. Kauffer saw a minute flaw in his assistant's copy and flew into a rage – a most unusual occurrence. In a fury he tore up not the enlargement but his own original. The poster was lithographed from the assistant's copy.

Surely to take poster design so seriously, to get into such a state about pieces of ribbon and invisible errors, surely all this seems faintly ludicrous? Perhaps it is, but perhaps it is best understood as an expression of Kauffer's frustration as a private man working in a very public medium. The importance he attached to work in the public sector is made clear in the address he gave to the Royal Society of Arts in 1938. Nothing much had changed technically, he thought, since the time of Lautrec, compared to another kind of change:

Our social background . . . has changed within thirty years almost beyond recognition. This has had its effect upon the artist, and a profound one, too. With the world as it is, and social values what they are, there is an almost inevitable tendency for thoughtful and creative people to seek sanctuary in a private world. I cannot help feeling myself that external reality has to some extent lost something of its collective significance, or perhaps it is that its significance seems less valuable and less immediate in its appeal, contrasted with the distress that social disruption on such a colossal scale as we have witnessed in our time, has created.[14]

In these circumstances – as Europe moved closer towards another war – Kauffer saw his work as a healing art, the more effective as it was part and parcel of ordinary business transactions. He even saw the enlightening commerce between artist and public as obstructed only by conscience-less, badly directed, commerce: and he went so far as to suggest that artists who did not work in advertising were – in the face of massive social dislocation – contributing nothing. (Presumably this was said in the heat of the moment – he would surely not have preferred Matthew Smith to flounder among problems of design which he himself handled with mastery – and yet his friend Kenneth Clark said almost as much in 1939: 'To be a pure painter seems almost immoral.')[15] Kauffer's words may seem 'extreme' but they may simply be visionary: undoubtedly they are utterly genuine.

The artist in advertising is a new kind of being . . . it is his business constantly to correct values, to establish new ones, to stimulate advertising and help to make it worthy of the civilisation that needs it.[16]

A NOTE ON TECHNIQUE

Kauffer published a short note on technique in the catalogue of an exhibition of his work held at the Museum of Modern Art, New York, in 1937 (about which more will be said in the next chapter):

. . . I have used all kinds of instruments common to most contemporary painters, such as tooth brushes, cheese cloth, wire netting, etc. – in fact anything that suggests interesting textures. The air-brush I seldom use now, but when I did use it a few years ago I realized that it was a tricky instrument and that its use required an exceedingly disciplined technique. At the moment I prefer methods less exacting and with more direct contact between my idea and the medium. Lithography still tends to be commercially practical for reproduction and most of my posters are done by an old firm still using in most cases actual lithograph stones.

A sponge-brush was a favourite tool, used for the illustrations to *Elsie and the Child*, for example. Tooth brushes were used to achieve a 'splatter' effect through a wire grid – this resembles air-brush technique at first glance but has a rougher, less machine-like, texture. Kauffer was probably referring to the Baynard Press when he mentioned lithograph stones (as opposed to zinc or aluminium sheets). At the Baynard Press the master craftsman Thomas Griffits was responsible for translating artists' originals into lithographic prints. Kauffer was fortunate in being the beneficiary of the first-class printing skills available at such printers as Baynard, Vincent Brooks Day & Son, Dangerfield, and Waterlow. Curwen, surprisingly, printed only one Kauffer poster. The subject was the Natural History Museum, commissioned by London Transport. It reached final proof stage in 1939 but was never printed – economic uncertainty and then war shut down commercial advertising, and Hans Schleger recalled how posters were covered over with black paper when rentals for hoarding space ran out and were not renewed. Kauffer's Natural History Museum poster was, however, eventually issued by London Transport in 1975.

Kauffer usually provided clients with two 'rough' designs for posters, often quite similar treatments. The one chosen was then enlarged in scale for printing. In the thirties Sidney Garrad was responsible for much of the work of enlargement, including the lettering. Kauffer's use of lettering has not won favour with typographers. He would not allow his assistant to adjust letter spacing, for example, to compensate for the inequalities of spacing inherent in letter forms. He also insisted on a number of incongruous distortions of letter forms in keeping with his own ideas of consistency – so that, for example, the horizontal bars of Ps and Rs defy good typographic usage. His early posters were Double Crown size (20 × 30 inches, or One Sheet). For these he provided same-size originals. After 1921 the Underground used the Double Royal size (25 × 40 inches), for which Kauffer made half-size scale originals. The Shell lorry bills, at 30 × 45 inches, were a special variation on the standard Quad Crown (30 × 40 inches) size. Kauffer's expertise included photography – he himself took the night photograph of the Horse Tamers in the Place de la Concorde, which he used in montage on *BP Ethyl Controls Horse-Power* (1933, plate 42). His albums of photographs are now in the Victoria and Albert Museum and the Cooper Hewitt Museum.

CHECKMATE 1937

Kauffer's designs for *Checkmate* form the climax of his work in the theatre. He had maintained contact with this medium by designing the stage settings and principal dresses for Ernest Milton's production of *Othello*, which opened at the St James's Theatre on 4 April 1932. Milton himself played the title role but was generally thought to have miscast himself – he lacked physical stature and presence and the play was soon taken off. Flora Robson's Bianca and Henry Oscar's Iago drew praise from James Agate, who felt that the production had been 'run away with by Miss Robson and Mr Oscar pounding neck and neck, with Mr McKnight Kauffer's beautiful scenery half a length behind'.[17] In the *Observer* Ivor Brown praised Kauffer's designs for their distinction and lack of 'selfconscious fuss'.[18] Little evidence survives to give a good idea of Kauffer's work for the play, although the sets were naturalistic, rather geometrical and low-key in colour.[19]

His next theatre work was for John Gielgud's production of a new play by Gordon Daviot, *Queen of Scots*, which opened at the New Theatre in St Martin's Lane on 8 June 1934. Gwen Ffrangcon-Davies played Mary Stuart, Laurence Olivier was the Earl of Bothwell and James Mason played a minor part. Kauffer contributed the scenery – which is austere in design and calculatedly crude in painted finish – and the principal men's costumes. Motley designed the dresses of the principal women. There was no relationship between the conventionally sumptuous historical costumes and the archaic austerity of the sets. The *Morning Post* critic found nothing to complain of in the contradiction of styles and described the production as 'a joy to the eye at every point, simple in stagery, gorgeous in costume'.[20] The *Sunday Times*, surprisingly, found the play 'too pretty. The fault is magnified by Mr McKnight Kauffer's smart scenery which is like the shop window of some ultra-modish decorator. The dresses are handsomer still, and one feels that the entire company might be going on to the costliest and most charitable ball.'[21] The play was widely noticed and generally well received but failed – unfortunately for Kauffer, whose fee of £20 was to have been augmented by a percentage of box-office receipts.

Kauffer's collaboration with Ninette de Valois and Arthur Bliss to create *Checkmate* in 1937 was his first and last triumph in the theatre. He had first worked with de Valois when he provided a special curtain used for a musical interlude (Walton's *Portsmouth Point* overture) in an evening of ballet arranged by the Camargo Society at the Savoy Theatre in 1932. Ninette de Valois, once a soloist in the Ballet Russe, filled a vacuum in ballet after Diaghilev's death in 1929. Her Vic-Wells Ballet company was founded in 1931, later taking the name of its home theatre as the Sadler's Wells Ballet. *Checkmate* was the production which marked the company's arrival at international stature. Bliss provided the book and score, de Valois the choreography, McKnight Kauffer the costumes and the two stage curtains required. The ballet was first given, as *Echec et Mat*, at the Théâtre des Champs Elysées in Paris on 15 June 1937. It was the first night of the season and the Vic-Wells Ballet had been taken to Paris by the British Council as part of the national contingent for the International Exhibition of that year. The cast for the first performance included June Brae as the Black Queen, Harold Turner as the First Red Knight, Robert Helpmann as the Red King, Pamela May as the Red Queen, William Chappell as the Second Red Knight, and Richard Ellis and Michael Somes as the Black Knights. The two chess players, Love and Death, who form a prologue to the ballet, were given by Frederick Ashton and Alan Carter. The *corps de ballet* included Margot Fonteyn (as a pawn).

Kauffer's curtain for the prologue was blue-grey in colour and

Checkmate (Love) 1937–46

decorated with a giant arm and hand, suggestive of an artificial limb operated by wires and pulleys. The isolated hand was a typical quasi-Surrealist feature of Kauffer's design repertoire in the thirties. Here it is aptly used to focus on the crucial moment about to be enacted in the game of chess between Love and Death. It is a visual magnification of the moment and a dramatization of the geometry of chess – but also perhaps implies an impersonally operating destiny. The curtain rises to reveal a giant chess board on which the dance of Love and Death is enacted. Kauffer's block-like costumes echo the geometry of the squares: red for the forces of love, grey-blue and black for the side of death. The dancing – Bliss said that de Valois 'moved the pieces like an Alekhine' – takes place before Kauffer's second curtain. This again made use of items from his basic stock of devices. He chose to adapt his space-frame convention – sets of parallel lines angled to imply sharp backward recession (or abrupt forward movement). These are linked with a sequence of four large-scale triangles, which are again tilted to imply movement. The shapes shift on different visual readings and in scale, angularity and colour provide a symbolic setting for the action: heroic, restless and intense. The Black Queen first seduces, then treacherously kills the Red Knight, and finally forces the Red King to submit to her will. The ballet critic Clive Barnes has singled out as the most striking visual images the entrance of the Red King and Queen, the funeral cortège of the Red Knight and 'the sudden twist of the body given by the Red King as he sees himself trapped by the inexorable Black forces'.[22]

The ballet was well received in Paris and in London, where it opened at the Sadler's Wells Theatre on 5 October 1937. Barnes has perceptively suggested that the theme must, in 1937, have carried with it 'political overtones (of which possibly even the composer and choreographer were unaware) greatly adding to the poignancy for contemporary audiences. Abyssinia, Austria, and later Czechoslovakia, all forced to their knees by the aggressive forces in Europe, probably gave a particular truthfulness to the Red King's tragedy.' This would have been much enhanced by Robert Helpmann's dancing, which an eye-witness of the performances in 1937 described as 'a tremendous performance of nervous terror that has never been approached by any of his successors'.[23] The ballet drew very large audiences and earned the admiration of Toscanini. All the sets and costumes were lost in Holland in May 1940 when the Vic-Wells Ballet was caught in the Hague by the German invasion. The company was able to make its way back to England in safety, but was obliged to leave behind the scenery, costumes and music for six ballets. Kauffer redesigned *Checkmate* – effectively streamlining his original conception – for its post-war revival at Covent Garden on 18 November 1947.[24]

THE WHITE HOUSE AT NORTH END

We *have* the cottage – Field can leave mid-May – we are so excited – too good to be true sort of feeling – so now we shall be neighbours

wrote Kauffer to Olivia Beddington on 14 April 1938. They had the lease of a charming, small Regency house in Buckinghamshire – the White House, North End – not far from the Beddingtons' country retreat at Turville Heath. The village of North End is a scatter of houses with a shop or two, some farms and a duck pond, eight miles from Henley-on-Thames in the Chiltern hills. The White House has a large garden with a wood behind it. This swoops down to a valley with cornfields laid out

Countryside at North End 1938–9
Photographs by Kauffer

The White House 1938–9
Photograph by Kauffer

among gentle knolls. They were pleased to discover that the proprietor of the village store was Harold Curwen. One thing still marked out the reformer of printing in his retirement job: the big drawers of flour, brown sugar and tapioca were labelled in a neat calligraphic hand learned from Edward Johnston thirty years before.[25] Kauffer took great interest in the house and extended the sitting-room and panelled it. He also converted an out-house into a studio. French windows looked out

Phoenix 1938–9 Photograph by Kauffer

on to newly planted shrubs, apple trees from an old orchard, and a handsome walnut tree. Away to the left was a paddock, a farm-house beyond that. Grass plots were laid out and bordered with bricks, vegetables put in, hedges planted.

The surrounding Buckinghamshire landscape made a great impression on Kauffer. Despite the growing certainty of war and scarcer commissions, the next two years were among Kauffer's happiest. He made many photographs down in the cornfields at harvest-time. It was in the valley below the wood that he saw a 'Phoenix' one day – at least that is what one of his photographs makes out of the simple ingredients of a corn-stook, a jacket and a stick. Something of this scene appears in his posters – *TVO–Draw Bar Pull*, an agricultural theme no doubt specially commissioned by Beddington in 1938, and two landscape posters for the Underground in the same year which are lyrical Buckinghamshire fields and woods. At every opportunity Kauffer and Marion would jump into their Packard car – with their silver cairn terrier Timsy – and make the quick journey from Chelsea to North End.

No sooner had Kauffer put down roots in the English countryside than war threatened to remove him from England altogether. On 5 June 1939 he sent his daughter Ann the present of Rimbaud's *Poesies* and wrote: 'Since the September crisis my work and work like mine has been very much cut down but I expect business will pick up again.'[26] A little later he wrote again. War had already been declared. 'My usual work has been stopped of course and unless I can get some other kind of work I shall be forced to go to America. In the meantime I am doing the tasks of an ordinary country labourer – and not minding it.' On 5 October he wrote: 'My work is dead for the moment, but here I work in the fields and vegetables and saw and chop wood.' They took an evacuee, a boy of 11.

On Christmas Day 1939 he reported to his daughter that he had been invited to New York, where a retrospective exhibition of his work at the Museum of Modern Art had brought him some reputation in 1937. He had an agent there eager to promote him and had already designed a series of covers for *Harper's Bazaar*. 'Work here is practically non-existent and I find when I do see heads of propaganda departments for the Government – I am appalled and disheartened by the triumph of the second-rate intelligence. All the jobs are occupied with inferior advertising "professionals" except one. I have seen Robert Bevan [son of the painter] at the Ministry of Information – I knew him as a young boy. He is the only one I have met who tries and will try to get something above the commonplace.'

Kauffer occupied himself reading Kierkegaard and Dante and tried his hand at illustrating the *Inferno*. He encouraged his daughter to think of the future. 'The war is awful and wasteful – yet if your generation can see it through – there will be a new world – a really new one this time for there is a new and strong desire of the people for spiritual values – such as was not apparent during and after the last war. No dear, its going to be a fine world – Truly.' He was given part-time employment at the Ministry of Information – poorly paid, but worse, a hack job which he felt his assistant there could do just as well. He wrote to Ann from the Ministry of Information on 19 June 1940: 'I understand from the U.S. Embassy that all American citizens will be considered liabilities if conditions become bad. I have made inquiries about work for your mother – no Americans can get work unless they do it voluntarily for American organizations. Whether I wish to leave England or not I more than likely will have to do so because of a means to earn a living which

Sandpiper and breaker 1938–40(?)
Pencil and water-colour

can not be expected to be obtained here.' His position was aggravated by a strange bureaucratic necessity which obliged him to obtain a travelling permit every time he travelled from Chelsea to North End. 'I do hope in any case' Eliot wrote to him on 5 June 1940, 'that the position will be dealt with sensibly, so that you do not need to get special permission to move between Chelsea and North End on each occasion.'[27]

The two men were on intimate terms by this time. On Easter Monday 1940 Kauffer wrote to congratulate Eliot on a newly published poem: 'Your greatness of spirit and humility have never been set down better than in "East Coker". It is difficult not to write to you without reverence – but it is a reverence of appreciation and thankfulness that you live and that you write and that we can read what you write.'[28] 'Now about the White House', Eliot replied, 'nothing would give me more anticipation of content than the prospect of another visit to Mr and Mrs Roosevelt. . . . May I come down after the middle of June?'[29] A little later he acknowledged the gift of a water-colour from Kauffer and confessed: 'I have imitated you and bought a pair of fawn corduroy trousers: but mine are only Daks.'[30] He came to North End for the weekend of 7–10 June 1940. At Kauffer's request he wrote a poem for use as a 'broadside' at a British photographic exhibition to be held later that year in New York, 'Britain at War'. Under the walnut tree Eliot composed 'Defence of the Islands'. He inscribed the original pencilled draft, now in the Pierpont Morgan Library: 'For Marion Dorn in remembrance of June 7–10 1940'. When he later collected the poem Eliot dedicated it to Kauffer's memory.

Already German raiders had appeared over Buckinghamshire and the Dunkirk evacuation had occurred. Eliot's moving poem is one long sentence which is almost of prose plain-ness, closing with the words:

> . . . to say, to the past and future generations
> of our kin and of our speech, that we took up
> our positions, in obedience to instructions.

Within a very short time of its completion, however, on 1 July 1940, Kauffer and Marion Dorn had left the country. The next day Peter Gregory began a diary:

On July 1st I suffered a great loss in the departure of Ted and Marion Kauffer: they returned to America on SS *Washington*, which sailed from Galway: they went at almost a moment's notice. The American Ambassador issued an intimation that the *Washington* would probably be the last boat to take back American citizens and that those who remained would become liabilities: so there was practically no alternative but for them to go. They only knew a few days beforehand and then they had to make hurried preparations ... they could only take such personal belongings as clothes and twenty-five pounds each.[31]

In retrospect the decision to leave seems to have been a mistake – a mistake serious enough in its consequences to be called tragic. Eliot had taken British citizenship, Kauffer had not – as an 'alien' he was not only subject to petty, misapplied regulations governing his movements, but also, it seems, not quite accepted at the Ministry of Information. As an alien he was paid on a fee rather than salary basis – at £3 3s a day.[32] This level of payment was not ungenerous. What disheartened Kauffer was the lack of intelligence and awareness at the Ministry. He felt that his assistant could do all the tasks which he himself was assigned – and when Kauffer left his assistant did take over the post. Marion was worried about family affairs in California. Kauffer felt that they were already – giving no real return in work for the valuable food and supplies they consumed – liabilities. New York seemed to want him. The decision was made. Hans Schleger rang the Swan Court flat by chance to be told by the maid that Kauffer and Marion Dorn were already on their way to the railway station en route for Ireland. Schleger hurried to the station. After Kauffer's death he wrote this account of the departure, which was also his final tribute to him:

On a dismal afternoon in 1940, I said goodbye to Ted Kauffer and Marion in a railway carriage – made smaller by Marion's harpsichord. We had been friends since we met.

Ted was an infinitely complex person. Known to the world by his austere and masculine work, friends knew his frail and sensitive inner being – clients loved his great charm and courage, feared his unwillingness to make concessions. He liked to smile and to tease his friends – yet he was an intense and serious man: he rarely designed a humorous poster. He was tender but remote . . . among designers: the 'First Gentleman'.

He loved England but remained American in fact and in feeling. As Laver said of Whistler, he had something of the potted plant, transferred but never transplanted.

Ted wanted to serve public rather than commercial interests – that is why he liked Jack Beddington's Shell and Frank Pick's and Christian Barman's Underground.

We lost his leadership during the war. He left because – impatiently mistaken – he believed himself suddenly unwanted. The shock felled him.

In America he did not find contact with his home soil – the plant had grown unaccustomed to the now foreign climate. He was a great and generous friend.[33]

Kauffer in New York studio 1940s Photograph © Arnold Newman

Chapter 7. **New York, 1940-54**

KAUFFER AND MARION DORN left nearly everything behind in England, down to the sheets on the beds. Peter Gregory took on their flat at Swan Court and the painter Hubert Wellington and his wife Irene (the distinguished calligrapher) took over the lease of the White House. It was not until 23 February 1941 that Kauffer wrote his first full letter back to Jack Beddington:

My dear Jack –
I should have written to you long ago though I did write you a letter thanking you for the notes to Resor and Cecil but it was a note and not a real letter. I have not seen either of the above yet! And I won't explain because it is too long and irrelevant.

I need not tell you that New York on extremely short rations (money) is no joke. By infinite scraping and working like hell on small jobs, anything that comes along, we have between us been able to eat (modestly and our own preparing) and to pay the rent. I have seen the winter through with a raincoat and one pair of shoes. I brought two pair suedes with me but these are like paper in the cold and snow so I bought a pair $10.49. You see I have a swell reputation but I have a 'European point of view' and the English point of view interesting as it is IS not the American point of view. So I have to 'build up' slowly again. I *will* do it, my teeth are set but it can't be done in a hurry.

Shortly after we arrived I did a job for N.W. Ayer for the Lincoln Continental car. Ayers were just losing the Ford account and the catalogue was so badly printed that as a job for getting others it was a washout and poorly paid to boot. During the last fortnight I have landed (again Ayer) some colour pages for The American Container Corporation, Fortune and Life ads – but this is a prestige job and not a money maker! So what! Bread and butter thin at times has been obtained by my doing bookjackets principally for

Donald Klopfer [of Random House] and Knopf.

Marion has been wonderful about the situation. She has worked every minute, peddled Seventh Avenue and made scarves. She too will come out on top but it's slow and we have no resources and honestly I would hate to try and borrow money in N.Y. at the present moment.

We see Marjorie quite frequently. She is beginning a new venture for designers and manufacturers. It opens in a fortnight. Marion is one of her headliners – no money yet! She is well and I like Mr Moss – we always speak lovingly of you – wonder what you are up to! She sends her love.

I have heard much about your films [Beddington was appointed director of the Ministry of Information films division in April 1940]. I must be frank and tell you that we have not been to a movie but once since we arrived. You see England is a touchy spot with us – we break down on the slightest provocation – we can't bear to think of her heroic spirit being put to such long and constant endurance. Any actual picture – God Save the King – or a voice on the air – Marion and I are reduced to sobs and despair, because we are not there – this is the reason. We live hermit lives because we feel that while England is in trial and suffering we can by being to ourselves be closer to the country and people we love so deeply and dearly.

The White House is sold. I don't know all the reasons why but finances I daresay are the main reasons and it was for these difficulties which were mounting higher and higher we thought it best to try our luck here and not get beyond recovery staying on in England. Had I felt myself to be indispensable at the Ministry I would most certainly have stayed on – but I could not honestly rationalize myself into believing that I was doing anything that my assistant who now fills the job could not do as well. With the sale of the White House went our most precious belonging. We loved this place – it was our first real home. Our other belongings, even my books, affected us not so deeply. In my sleep and in quiet moments of the day I walk the lovely lanes of Buckinghamshire and I seee the beechwoods and now the tiny wild flowers and soon the lanes will be busy with nesting.

England will have a beautiful spring again, of this we are all certain, maybe not this one but again for a certainty. It will be renewed in greatness and it will shine again as it did in Queen Elizabeth's day and we here in this new country will envy the growth that has been made through suffering, and endurance such as the world has never seen. We admire Mr Churchill – his is the voice of England both in meaning and in beauty. He is the real statue of liberty which the people of Britain have made. England is truly the light of the civilised world. God bless England.

I have tears in my eyes, I have a longing to be with you all, a longing that will *never die*.

I love America too but in a different way. It is an objective attachment perhaps and I would have to live here for a long time to feel any intimacy such as I felt so much in England. I love our concept of liberty, I love the clear light and the vast sense of space. I admire our history and our fight for some of the essential rights of man. Our figures in history such as Washington, Jefferson, Lincoln, our men of letters like Franklin, Emerson, Whitman, Poe and many others inspire me with hope and ambition, but I am very sad.

New York streets are lonely I think and I have seen so many people with a homeless kind of expression. This is new to me for you never see that in London.

Dearest Jack. It is now March 2nd! I must get this off to you – quickly – on the next 'Clipper'. There is so much to tell you, yet it all seems so remote from the real thing that is going on in the world. So much stupidity in America: people literally do not know – do not take the trouble or have the interest in finding out *what* the world that loves freedom is up against. I hear their remarks and I beat my head with anguish. If suffering brings understanding – then America must suffer to gain greater capacity to understand.

No day goes by – hardly an hour – the last thing at night – the first thing in the morning – our thoughts are of England.

March 6th

Time passes – another few days since I last tried to finish this letter. It must go – now even though I have left so much unsaid. But I will write soon again and fill the gap.

Have you built the brick wall in the garden? I can see it all and now so many things will be showing their green faces. We give Olivia our devoted love and to the children too. Marion sends love – my affection and love to you – I miss not seeing you – but all our lives are now different so very different – England – beloved England –

Devotedly,

Ted

P.S. Joe [Blumenthal? of Spiral Press] sends most affectionate greetings – I will write to you about the 'big shots' in New York designing and tell you how they do not design at all! Its a wonderful racket. I look on in rapt amazement. I now know what's wrong with U.S. design. – Ted

'21' is out of my class, so I can give you no news of your favourite haunt. My best wishes, please, to Miss Spendlove, Vernon Nye and John B. Oh dear, why am I exiled *now*!

Write soon.

Tell Sidney, I shall send a $5 note when the war is over this summer – and give him fondest good wishes from us both – Ted.[1]

Kauffer unburdened himself to his close friend Beddington but he wrote in better order to Colin Anderson a little earlier (10 February 1941):

What seems so strange is that I am here at all. I never imagined myself anywhere except in England – yet I would not become naturalized – a strange conflict. But I think I do know why – simply told it is this – I am an American from the West – no matter how strongly I feel about England, how much I should like to belong to England I could only do so so far. In other words I could not become English because it isn't in my bone and heritage and as I would only be part instead of whole as I should like to have been. . . .

Except for a visit to the Planetarium, the Metropolitan Museum and the Natural History Museum I have hardly moved out of the radius between 46th Street and 60th and across a matter of six American 'blocks' and they are very short. I work every minute – I have none of my work here, either originals or reproductions. So I've had to make a portfolio of work. My European reputation which preceded me by a few years has definitely stamped me as English. This is not a criticism with material inference – but a difference of 'advertising thinking'. The American advertiser respects the European achievement but in no way will he admit it in American practice – so I've got to wear that off! I've got to show them. Shall I be able to do it? My American youth may now be useful at last!

Our winter light is clear, cold and bright. The towering buildings stand out so solid against an infinite blue sky with puffs of white clouds passing on to other frontiers – perhaps to the South where it is warm or perhaps to the West where they will float slowly across deserts and finally rest on the peaks of the Rockies. Wherever you are in America there is always a beyond – the seas are too far from each other and the Mississippi is too long for one to ever stop.

The Museum of Modern Art have just opened a very comprehensive exhibition of American Indian Art – sculpture, pottery, some painting, costume and implements. Here is a rich, virile background for Americans to take stock of. It is very Picasso, it is very Chinese, it is even Brancusi – it is not violent like Aztec art. It is in most cases highly sensitive to texture, purpose and use. It is the most stimulating evidence I have seen of an American art. . . .[2]

Kauffer was on very friendly terms with Alfred H. Barr Jr and Monroe Wheeler of the Museum of Modern Art. His 'Britain at War' exhibition was first shown in the British Pavilion at the New York World Fair in the autumn of 1940. The following year it became a Museum of Modern Art

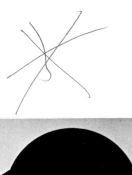

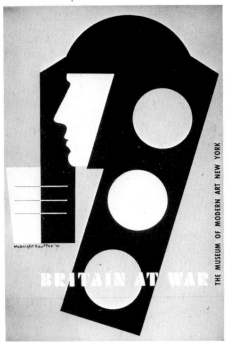

Britain At War 1941
Exhibition catalogue cover

exhibition and book – with a cover designed by Kauffer. In 1941 he also designed the cover of the Museum's exhibition catalogue *Organic Design*. Barr had introduced Kauffer's work to the American public in 1937 with an exhibition of 85 posters, which later travelled to other museums in the United States. This was only the second one-man exhibition the Museum had given a poster artist (Cassandre was the first to be so honoured), and the occasion was given added distinction by Aldous Huxley's introduction to the exhibition catalogue. Huxley defined the kind of advertising with which Kauffer was embattled in London and then New York:

Most advertising artists spend their time elaborating symbols that stand for something different from the commodity they are advertising. Soap and refrigerators, scent and automobiles, stockings, holiday resorts, sanitary plumbing and a thousand other articles are advertised by means of representations of young females disporting themselves in opulent surroundings. Sex and money – these would seem to be the two main interests of civilized human beings.

For Huxley, Kauffer's value lay in his use of a rather different type of symbolism – 'the symbols with which he deals are not symbols of something else; they stand for the particular things which are under consideration.'

Eliot wrote on 29 August 1941 giving news of mutual friends, mentioning in passing his fire-watching duties at Faber and Faber, and apologizing for the long silence:

I wish I might have some direct news from you or Marion, but so far I have not deserved it. It must have been very difficult for you to make the decision to leave, but I can well understand and sympathise with the reasons, and I think it was the best thing to do. I have no doubt that the problem of adaptation to New York has been very trying too.[3]

There was no reply to the letter until Marion Dorn wrote back to Eliot on 14 December. Kauffer had had a breakdown during the summer. Marion wrote:

The doctors can talk all they want about germs and viruses, but I knew he wasn't tough enough to meet New York. He dreamed about Lincoln's America and the pioneers, and I remember telling Eric once all about Ted's vision of America, and how the thought of his coming here frightened me.[4]

Kauffer momentarily lost his nerve. In the extreme competitiveness of New York advertising he found it difficult to sell work because, Marion wrote, he was no longer confident enough to sell himself. Fortunately, Marion came into some family money, and they were able to establish themselves in a grand flat overlooking Central Park at 40 Central Park South. The apartment was more opulent than their previous quarters, but bare of decoration except for lots of house plants and a Quattrocento angel in a painted blue robe.[5]

In October 1941 Kauffer was represented in an exhibition at the Katharine Kuh Gallery, Chicago, called 'The Advance Guard of Advertising Artists' – with Frank Barr, Lester Beall, Gyorgy Kepes, Herbert Matter, Moholy-Nagy, Paul Rand, and Ladislav Sutnar. The exhibition was also shown at the A–D Gallery, New York, in the following March. On 26 November 1941 he addressed the Art Directors' Club of New York.[6] He opened with a quotation from C.H. Waddington's book *The Scientific Attitude*: 'The true, or at least the most important, task of the cultural worker is to reveal to man the spiritual riches which result from the full exploitation of the immediate, practical possibilities.' He went on to make two points which he was to make on many future occasions. The first was that American businessmen were, in general, remote from contact with their designers compared to their English counterparts. He later wrote of the 'in-between world of research, rationalization and sales-talk' which divided client and designer.[7] His second point was that American advertising was not ambitious enough in relation to its political and literary heritage and the grandeur of its natural environment: 'Does it compete or throw into relief anything of this big scene?'

Perhaps inevitably, Kauffer's reputation remained a rather esoteric one and his commissions for posters came mainly from institutions. He designed institutional magazine advertisements for the Container Corporation and American Silk Mills, war posters for Asuntos Interamericanos, the Greek War Relief Association, Friends of Greece, Inc., American Friends of Norway, the Office of Civilian Defense, the C.A.A. War Training Service, the United Committee of South Slavic Americans, the United C.I.O. War Relief Committee and the American Red Cross (see plates section). Of his poster *Steel! Not Bread* (a bayoneted hand) Kauffer said: 'America has been trying to sell the war to the public with pretty legs and bosoms. War is grim and you have to be grim to win.' The poster was designed for the U.S. War Bond Drive and in 1943 Kauffer was honoured by the U.S. Treasury Department for 'distinguished service in the War Savings Program'.

Magazine advertisement for American Silk Mills 1940s Gouache

The 1945 Red Cross contribution campaign was heralded by Kauffer's *Give* poster. The design featured a blue-black background with a white arrow pointing diagonally downward to the simple one-word message GIVE (see plate 68). The small red cross in the white arrow was the focal colour spot. Millions of copies of this poster were printed in a variety of different sizes, down to postcards. They were distributed for posting on wall panels, sides of lorries, bulletin boards in schools, churches and public buildings, in the interiors of trains, buses and stores, as well as on giant outdoor hoardings on highways and city streets. The design was no doubt a potent factor in the highly successful Red Cross appeal.[8] Kauffer received a 'Certificate of Honor' from the American Red Cross in 1945.

Other clients included Barnum and Bailey's Circus, and the New York Subways Advertising Co Inc. For the New York Subway Kauffer produced a design on a theme dear to his heart – a minimal indication of a clown's face with the text *Subway Posters Perform Daily Before Five Million Pairs of Eyes*, devised for a campaign in 1947–8. The design won the Art Director of the job, Jefferson Tester, an Award for Distinctive Merit from the Art Directors' Club of New York. It appeared as poster, mailing piece and magazine advertisement and was shown in exhibitions of contemporary American poster art in Vienna and Japan. In 1947 Kauffer became Honorary Advisor to the Department of Public Information of the United Nations. A commission from the Container Corporation gave him especial pleasure. He was asked to contribute an image of Montana for a series of full-colour magazine pages depicting every state in the Union, commissioned by the Corporation in 1945–6. When contact with Eliot was resumed after the war Kauffer liked to call him Missouri (Eliot was born in St Louis) and to be called 'Montana' in return.[9]

In addition to these institutional commissions Kauffer was busy with the designs of scores of book jackets – for his old friend Alfred Knopf, the

Modern Library, Harcourt Brace, Random House, Pantheon Books and other companies. For Knopf he illustrated Langston Hughes's book *Shakespeare in Harlem*, a congenial task as he was fond of Harlem and its Negro population.[10] At a public meeting of the Committee on Art Education of the Museum of Modern Art in April 1948 Kauffer spoke as follows:

New forms of education, social problems of adjustment, racial discrimination and the Negro problem for which there is now an urgent necessity for intelligent and human cooperation, the activities of municipal public services, state problems and finally national problems, all of these need the services of intelligent thinkers, capable writers and the best designers.[11]

Books and their illustration were, however, to take up more of his time than his typical milieu of poster art (apart from one significant exception which we shall come to). The illustrations for *Shakespeare in Harlem* are unhatched line drawings which were reversed to make white drawings on a black ground – by this means they relate well in visual 'weight' to the letterpress of Hughes's poetry.

Bennett Cerf of Random House invited Kauffer to illustrate W.H. Hudson's pantheistic story *Green Mansions*, which Kauffer had admired since first reading Hudson in the early twenties. The charm of Kauffer's illustrations is not fully suggested by the colour lithography of the published book (1945). A more satisfactory result was achieved in the two-volume illustrated edition of Edgar Allan Poe published by Knopf in 1946. Kauffer contributed 10 illustrations which were reproduced by colour offset lithography, and a number of line vignettes. He had wanted to illustrate Poe since Eliot had introduced him to the story *The Assignation* in 1929.[12] Dr Desmond Flower has singled out Kauffer's portrait of Poe as the finest of the illustrations: 'Poe's hopelessness and slow disintegration are wonderfully suggested, and it is an unhappy thought that the poignancy of this design may have sprung from Kauffer's own bewildered state at that time.'[13] The work on Poe may even have contributed to Kauffer's feeling of isolation in New York. This was professional isolation rather than personal – but Kauffer had become used to a happy mixture of client/friends.

Some time in 1947 Kauffer became acquainted with a young man who fulfilled his hopes of what advertising might be in America, and also provided him with the same intimate professional friendship he had enjoyed with Peter Gregory and Jack Beddington. Bernard Waldman remembers looking up from his desk one day to receive his first impression of a new designer who had come to see him. Waldman was used to hearing the quick rattle of self-promotion and seeing a portfolio persuasively opened. He saw an exceedingly tall, very thin man, with a book under his arm. Craning forward, Waldman could hardly hear the man's soft voice. Here was someone who was decidedly not of Madison Avenue, hardly – the young man thought – of this world.

Waldman commissioned a poster, *Fashions in Flight*. Bold, determined and convinced of Kauffer's ability, he took a calculated risk:

After Ted made the poster for 'Fashions in Flight' I tried to interest American Airlines in having him do some of their posters. I was so sure that they would be well received that I suggested to American Airlines that I go on a trip with Ted and then submit the posters on speculation. In other words, if American Airlines did not like them they would not have to accept them – but I was so sure they would.

Our first visit was to Los Angeles, where the local sales manager recom-

Portrait of Poe 1946 Book illustration

Kauffer and Bernard Waldman (about 1950)

mended what he called the 'sun countries' – California, Nevada, Arizona, New Mexico.

Ted and I went to Las Vegas and as soon as we got there it was a completely changed man that I saw. Here was the America he loved and felt a part of. We did not stay too long in the city but travelled to the desert and to the mountains. We then went to Arizona – Phoenix, Tombstone, etc.

Ted was rejuvenated, revitalized and happy as I had never seen him before.

I had to return to New York and he stayed on a couple of weeks longer. Two or three months later he made the posters and American Airlines accepted them enthusiastically.

Ted was in his proper environment. For weeks, months and years he talked about the West, which to him was America rather than New York City which he called a depressing canyon of mortar, steel, bricks and glass.[14]

The series of posters is Kauffer's finest and most extensive from his New York period and continued until 1953. Here his lyrical landscape gift and his subtle colour sense re-asserted themselves. In 1947 he also redesigned the curtains and costumes for *Checkmate* which was revived at Covent Garden on 18 November 1947. The new designs follow the originals in general character but improve upon them by removing unnecessary mannerisms of Kauffer's earlier style (such as the cloud wisps he transferred directly from his posters to the costumes).[15] The main act curtain was also effectively simplified. The 1947 designs are those still used in this often revived ballet, which continues to be a popular item in the repertory of the Royal Ballet Company at Covent Garden.

Kauffer's influence continued to be felt by English designers after the war, perhaps partly because of *Checkmate*. The Festival of Britain symbol designed in 1950–51 by one of his most enthusiastic admirers, Abram Games R.D.I., is perhaps the last notable echo of Kauffer's style in England. *Checkmate* was given its New York première at the Metropolitan Opera House on 2 November 1949. Kauffer held a concurrent exhibition of his original designs for the ballet and his illustrations for Edgar Allan Poe at the American British Art Galleries in New York. His personal distinction had soon won him a circle of friends in America, including the humorist S.J. Perelman and the poets St John Perse and Marianne Moore. The latter wrote an introduction to Kauffer's exhibition which is as eloquent as any he

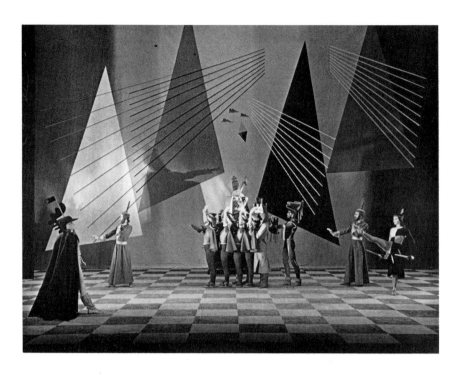

Checkmate
1971–2 revival by Royal Ballet Company

ever received and exemplary of its author's prose style:

E. McKnight Kauffer is a very great artist. Instinctiveness, imagination, and the 'sense of artistic difficulty' with him, have interacted till now we have an objectified logic of sensibility as inescapable as the colours refracted from a prism. Mr Kauffer's posters, book-jackets, and illustrations, partake of one attitude which is affirmative in all directions, so that here if nowhere else in the world, 'street art' is art. Shadows are as arresting as objects; numerals and letters are so rare in themselves that opposing angles, contrasting sizes, and basic parallels, are of consummate elegance – the only kind of eloquence not intrusive. This language of blacks and greys is colour in the sense that Chinese brush masterpieces are colour. Literal colour, moreover, rivals the acetylene blue of the cotinga and the tones in the beak of a toucan. We have here a poetry of synonyms like 'the immediate meaning and possible meaning' of poetry, as where a Mexican hat has the form of a plane, the heroism of helplessness is symbolized by a Greek child, and 'the medieval tower is half castle and half castle in the air'.

E. McKnight Kauffer is a parable of uncompromise – a master of illusion, focussing scrutiny upon the crease and curl of a Stetson, or on the firm solidity of a winter apple, verifying Democritus's axiom, 'Compression is the first grace of style.'

'What is to be more feared than death?' the man asked; the sage replied 'Disillusion'. Here, actually, we have a product in which unfalsified impulse safeguards illusion!

Marianne Moore also caught and preserved – embedded in one of her own poems – the precision, delicacy and deliberation of Kauffer's speaking voice. She used a passage remembered from his conversation to open her poem *The Icosasphere*, which was presumably written in or soon after 1950:

> In Buckinghamshire hedgerows
>   the birds nesting in the merged green density,
>   weave little bits of string and moths and feathers and thistledown,
>   in parabolic concentric curves. . . .

On one occasion Marianne Moore sent Kauffer a $10 bill and strict instructions to go out and buy himself a good dinner. Her tender, sisterly concern for him is also expressed in a note found inside his copy of Valéry's *Selected Writings* (which he lent to her in 1950): 'You really are safe; I am not disturbed about you and enviable of your height if only you could just realize it.' On another occasion she pronounced that 'Edward's jaws should be pryed open like the jaws of an elderly mule – and a great big pill called "Joy" should be forced down his throat.' Kauffer marked two passages in his copy of Valéry: 'Page 93: (I am) "in sum, the effect of an incalculable dis-order".' 'Page 97: "We are deceived by what is definite".' On the back of this note there is a sketch for a poster with a drawing of the globe and the words WORLD TRAVEL and Fly.[16]

Kauffer took great pleasure in the literary aspirations of Bernard Waldman's young daughter Grace, who is now a poet of international reputation and remains mindful of his kindness to her, and loyal to his memory:

He introduced me to the best books I read, such as Paul Valéry's poems and essays, *The Cantos*, Lu Chi's *Wen Fu* in translation, Stendhal's *On Love*. He loved those books, and shared the things he loved generously with me and my parents. I remember that he was very wise, but with humour in every gesture – as when I asked him to recommend a book that would help me to be a better writer and he presented me with a good dictionary (which I still have).[17]

In 1968 she received a letter from Marianne Moore saying 'I wish Edward Kauffer could see that his ambition for you was not misplaced.'

Kauffer continued to take pleasure in the American classics, in the landscape of the South-West, and in solving interesting problems of design. In Emerson he found the remark 'We eat and drink and wear perjury and fraud in a hundred commodities' and wondered: could Emerson have been thinking prophetically of what was to come? He continued to insist that advertising could be a healing, not a destructive, art:

The daily life of a citizen is punctuated with slogans, pictures, stops and go's. It is logical to assume that the mind welcomes and responds to any symbol or interpretation that expresses a sense of order, and good design is exactly concerned with this elementary and always compelling fact.[18]

He revisited the South-West in 1950 and called it 'a good kind of reality' – 'robust, uncomplicated, direct', with brilliant light and great spaces. Quixotically he bought a horse and left it in Arizona in the care of a cowboy called Jesse Crick. He carried a photograph of Crick and the horse in his wallet and liked the link he had established with that spectacular and inspiring country.[19] Eliot wrote to him that his friends were alarmed by the effect that New York had on him: 'Your friends here would like you back . . . I should feel happier about you in Chelsea – or in Arizona.'[20] Returning to New York in the war, as Kauffer had done, Man Ray said 'it meant joining the ranks of those whose greatest thrill consisted of buying and selling, if I wished to survive.'[21] He escaped to California to teach.

Friends have spoken of a sense of guilt which kept Kauffer from returning to England, as if he had betrayed his adopted country.[22] His feelings on the subject were deep and complex. In 1950, cheered by his visit to the South-West, he spoke enthusiastically of his return and its great possibilities:

America has a profuse variety of cultural and racial backgrounds. The people, despite our traditions of Puritanism and pragmatism, are romantic and

imaginative, responsive to the drama of presentation. Those qualities find little satisfaction in the safe, literal forms advertising has adopted. It is a country of intense light and dark contrasts, a wide, rich canvas against which to work. The possibilities for broadening communication through the graphic arts, in this country, are limitless.[23]

In the very same year, however, he wrote to Jack Beddington that 'Some kind of buried masochism drove me insanely back [to America] – and now I am reaping the "pay-off".' He dwells in the letter on his favourite Buckinghamshire lanes and breaks off with: 'Oh, my dear Jack – I must not think of it – Do you see what I mean?'[24] To Christian Barman, in the same year, Kauffer wrote:

Advertising is 'streamlined' according to the dictates of high-powered agencies and the lack of adventure to say nothing of imagination is deplorable. I am disillusioned and really sick of it all. Apart from the practical side i.e. making a living the whole thing has had a devastating effect on the psychological side and my bewilderment so often experienced has at times alarmed me. I have to say the least been driven into a corner and my talent for whatever it is worth thrown into the ash can.[25]

Kauffer's friends have sometimes insisted that his work never had any correlation with his day-to-day life, and this is no doubt true. On the other hand, there are occasions when his most imaginative inventions seem to correspond with what is known of him biographically. *Flight*, for example, remained a special talisman for Kauffer, and in the forties he illustrated it in a pamphlet which expressed his views on the potential of advertising art.[26] It is not difficult to find a connection between his most famous design and the characteristic movement of his mind – ardent, forward-looking, aspiring and even visionary in his flights of fancy for what might be. Perhaps the most original and compelling design of his American period is a jacket he designed for a book of poems by St John Perse, *Exile* (1949). The illustration is light on dark and consists of a simple graphic treatment of the 'X' in Exile. The crossed arms roam free of the island of the word, one hard, straight and rapid in movement, the other leisurely, hand-drawn, exploring beyond the border of the sheet. To the opposition of light and dark is added the simple opposition of the lines. There is possibly a suggestive link with a passage in Eliot's 'Burnt Norton', which Kauffer would have known well:

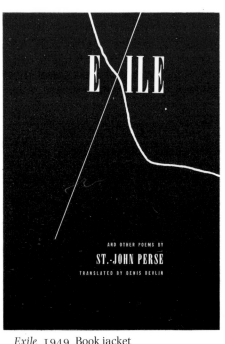

Exile 1949 Book jacket

> Words strain,
> Crack and sometimes break, under the burden,
> Under the tension, slip, slide, perish,
> Decay with imprecision, will not stay in place,
> Will not stay still . . . .

No subject could have roused Kauffer's deepest feelings so much as the idea of exile. He was exiled not only from England but also from the America he cherished as an ideal and for which he had found the physical evidence in the South-West. He was exiled from his wife Grace and daughter Ann in England. It is only one of many reflections that the *Exile* design inspires, that the arms of the X correspond in detail to the two country roads which meet at the White House at North End – an observation which came from Ann's husband Peter Rendall as soon as he saw the design. With Kauffer, whose best work is a subtle and layered synthesis, such an ingredient is by no means to be ruled out.

A daybook kept by Kauffer at this period records favourite memories of North End – the wild flowers along the hedgerows, the cat coming in

T.S. Eliot and Kauffer in New York
1940s

the evening to sip milk from its saucer – and unhappy reflections on his real environment:

If it is true that our teeth are whiter – our breath sweeter – our smoking cooler and our drinking more 'high class' – the gain is of doubtful value compared to what we lose in civilizing values – so far as the eye and mind are traduced. After the rest brought by sleep we awaken fresh – but only for a moment and then the day brings its fearful anxieties.[27]

As Kauffer began to lose interest in the New York advertising scene, Marion Dorn – on the other hand – was achieving success. Her work awaits a full appraisal, but important commissions included an interior scheme for Lockheed Airport, Los Angeles and she contributed to a White House carpet which featured emblems of all of the States in the Union. She adapted better to the demands of New York City and continued to produce high-quality work. Unfortunately the disparity between her success and Kauffer's exacerbated difficulties between the couple – and although they married at City Hall in 1950 they lived increasingly separate lives.[28]

Kauffer's loyal friend and most effective partner in the New York years, Bernard Waldman, has said that Kauffer chose to kill himself with drink, that it was a form of suicide. He continued to work to the end, almost obsessively, spending weeks on lettering that could have been left to an assistant. 'Poor Ted', wrote Mrs Waldman to her daughter, 'he has emptied his life of everything but his work and when that fails him he is lost.' His old friends Frank and Mary Dobson visited him in 1953 and found him 'still his old sweet self, but already a very sick man'. On 10 July 1954 Kauffer was admitted to hospital, made a recovery, but then had a final relapse. On 13 October Aldous Huxley wrote to Ann that her father was in Lenox Hill Hospital, 'desperately ill and in great pain, kidneys and liver being affected. Emaciation is extreme and it will take him a long time to get back to anything like normal health – if he *does* get back; for I judge that he is still in danger. I saw him last spring for the first time in several years and was shocked by his appearance even then. He was evidently working up for the crisis of this summer.'

Kauffer died on 22 October 1954. Huxley wrote to Ann on 10 November: 'Poor Ted – his last years were dreadfully unhappy, and he had reached a point where it seemed psychologically impossible for him to do anything that would in any way lessen his unhappiness. I think of him with affection and a kind of helpless pity – for there seemed to be nothing one could do to help him.'

Marion Dorn wrote to Eliot on 31 October. She told him how Kauffer's past life had seemed to fall away until he was simply 'Edward Kauffer' and of his intense fear at the end. 'I felt that he didn't want us – not any of us – that only his fear was real.' Eliot wrote back on 7 November with all the fine-grained sympathy one would expect of him. He also made this penetrating observation:

I think the fear has some obscure connection with not loving life, paradoxical as it may seem. I believe that something had left him, some years ago; and that all the external troubles, physical and spiritual, were perhaps merely attempts to find an objective reason for something for which no reason can be found, because it is simply the Void. . . .[29]

Eliot had, perhaps, constructed his life and his healing art of poetry over just such a void. Evidence of it appears in his plays as well as his poems. He once compared the role of an artist in advertising with that of a poet in the theatre who must 'aim to write a play that will please theatre-goers who neither know nor care about poetry, and he must try to write it in verse that will win the approval of poetry lovers who care nothing for the theatre'.[30] From *The Family Reunion*:

Now I know that all my life has been a flight
And phantoms fed upon me while I fled.

Marion Dorn asked Marianne Moore to write to Eliot about everything that had happened in the last weeks. She wrote on 27 October:

I can *not*, Tom; but can say this – I was aware above everything, of the love Edward had inspired – of the wondering reverence for him. . . . Service so touchingly, so privately, rendered Edward day by day.

Unselfative Nancy [Nancy Reid, who chose the music for the funeral service]. Bernard Waldman let nothing keep him from supplying certain necessities Edward would scarcely ask for; said 'I assure you, Miss Moore, he lacked for nothing'; was with him daily, a silent self-effacing man like Nancy.[31]

The service was held at the Campbell Chapel, at 81st Street and Madison Avenue, and Kauffer was buried in Woodlawn cemetery. His friend Sabro Hasigawa, a teacher at the New School of Social Research, had brought to the hospital a large white square of paper inscribed in Japanese brush characters: 'May the sun be in your heart.' To the grave Hasigawa brought a folded paper bird, bearer of the soul.

Plates

1

2

3

Soaring to Success !

DAILY HERALD

— the Early Bird.

LONDON HISTORY AT THE
LONDON MUSEUM
DOVER STREET
OR ST. JAMES'S PARK STATION

5

WINTER SALES
are best reached by
UNDERGROUND

6

WINTER
SALES
ARE BEST REACHED
BY
UNDERGROUND

7

MUSEUM OF
NATURAL
HISTORY
SOUTH KENSINGTON

8

9

EXHIBITION
OF
MODERN PAINTING AND SCULPTURE BY
THE LONDON GROUP
APRIL 12   MAY 17

MANSARD
GALLERY
HEAL & SON LTD.
TOTTENHAM COURT ROAD
10 A.M. to 6 P.M.   OPEN SATS.
ADMISSION 1 SHILLING
BOOK TO   GOODGE ST.

10

WINTER SALE
at DERRY
& TOMS
KENSINGTON W. 8

11

A TOWN
THAT IS
PLANNED

A HOME
TO BE
PROUD OF

GARDEN CITY
LESS THAN AN HOUR FROM
PICCADILLY CIRCUS
(via KINGS CROSS)
64 FINSBURY PAVEMENT, E.C.2 or
ESTATE OFFICE, WELWYN GARDEN CITY, HERTS.

12

13

14

15

16

17

18

E McKnight Kauffer, 24
"first thing every morning"
ENO'S
"FRUIT SALT"

MINING

TO HIDDEN TREASURE · Mining, the Open Sesame of the Modern World. Winning the earth's mineral wealth for the service, comfort, and enrichment of mankind · a thrilling romance. At the Empire Exhibition see and study it all. See how coal is got, how gold and diamonds are won. It is there to the life · the whole romance of mining.

BRITISH EMPIRE EXHIBITION

20

THE TRAVELLING PLAYERS ARE COM- -ING

PLAYS
MIMING
DANCING
FOLKSONGS

VARIETY
GAIETY
COLOUR
FANTASIES

THE ARTS LEAGUE TRAVELLING THEATRE

WILL BE AT

PLAYS, FANTASIES ENGLISH AND CELTIC FOLK-SONGS

21

EVERYWHEN FOR INDOOR AND OUTDOOR WEAR

"CRÊPE RUB BER SOLES"

C. & J. CLARK LIMITED

STREET SOMERSET

22

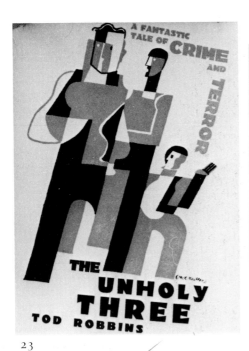

23

24

25

26

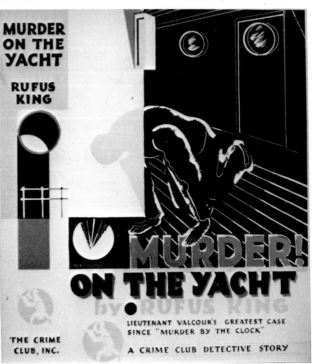

27

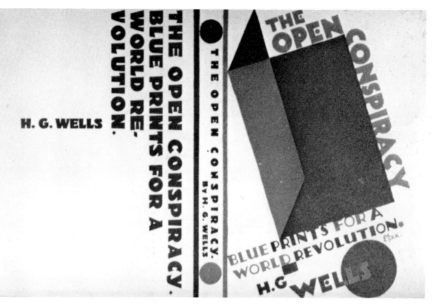

28

29

30

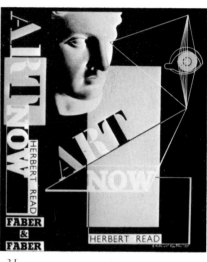

31

32

33

34

36

37

39

38

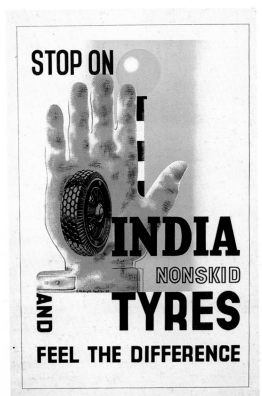

STOP ON

INDIA

NONSKID

AND TYRES

FEEL THE DIFFERENCE

40

NEW

SHELL

LUBRICATING

OILS

41

BP ETHYL

ANTI-KNOCK

CONTROLS HORSE-POWER

42

POWER

THE NERVE CENTRE OF LONDON'S

UNDERGROUND

43

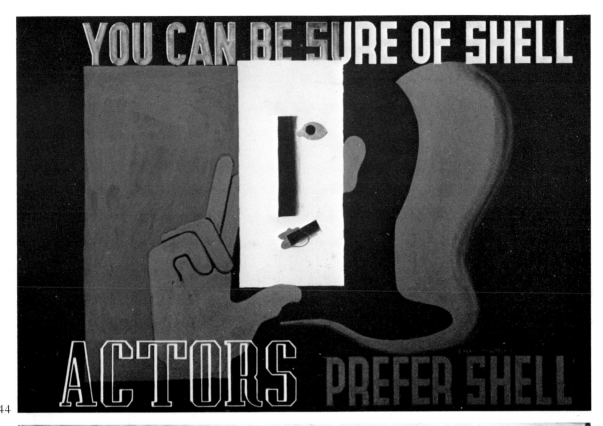

44

45

46

47

48

49

50

TRAVEL IN COMFORT BY IMPERIAL AIRWAYS

EUROPE AFRICA INDIA AND THE EAST

51

CONTACT WITH THE WORLD USE THE TELEPHONE

PRD 6 52

OCTOBER 14TH TO 23RD MOTOR SHOW

EARLS COURT

EARLS COURT

STATION ★ EARLS COURT
BUSES ★ 30·74

53

CHEAPER

EMPIRE

TELEGRAMS

ORDINARY FULL RATE 1s. 3d. A WORD
LETTER TELEGRAMS 5d. A WORD [minimum 25 words]

HAND IN YOUR TELEGRAM
HERE

54

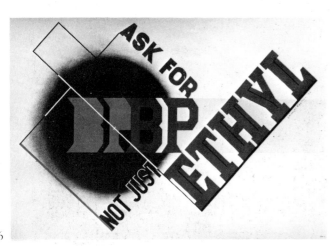

56

57

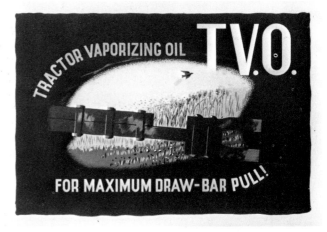

59

58

VISIT YOUR MUSEUMS

NATURAL HISTORY MUSEUM

WEEKDAYS 10 TO 6
SUNDAYS 2.30 TO 6
ADMISSION FREE

 STATION - SOUTH KENSINGTON

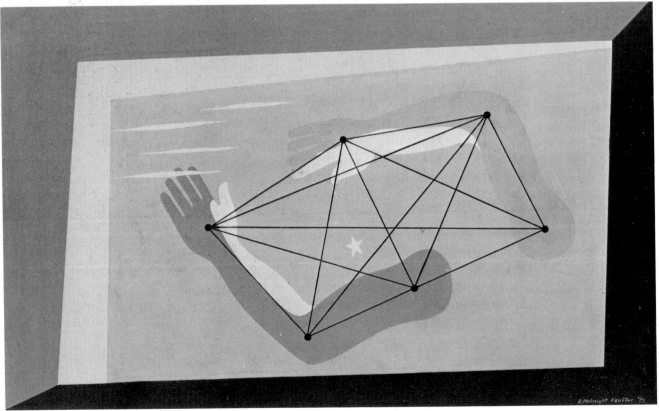

63

64

65

66

1942

67

68

RED CROSS WAR FUND

GIVE

Keep your **RED CROSS** at his side

69

SUBWAY POSTERS

PERFORM

DAILY BEFORE FIVE MILLION PAIRS OF EYES

70

71

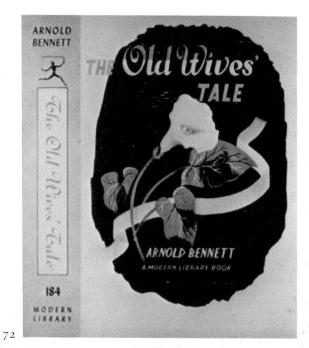

72

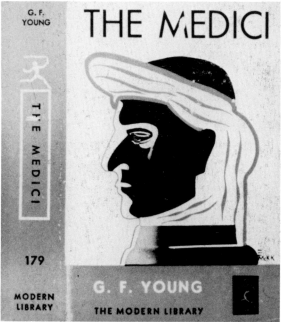

73

74

75

Notes

Chapter 1: The Californian

1. Kauffer's mother wrote down the history of the family for her son and the manuscript has been preserved by Mr Bernard Waldman, New York City.
2. Information given to the author by the late Maria Zimmern Petrie in 1970. Further information is to be found in her unpublished autobiography *Yesterday*, a copy of which is with her grandson Mr Brian Petrie, London.
3. 'E. McKnight Kauffer, Poster Designer', *Portfolio*, vol. 1, 1950, pp. 20–35.
4. The City Directory lists Ed. L. Kauffer as painter in 1907, scenic artist in 1908, and artist in 1909. Although his name was recorded at birth in the Cascade County records as Edward Kauffer the artist later added the family name Leland. I am grateful to Mr William A. Gumberts of Evansville Museum of Arts and Science for checking the Directory listings.
5. Article in *Portfolio*, op. cit.
6. The painting is in a private collection, London. A head and shoulders portrait of Kauffer, also by Armfield, is in the National Portrait Gallery, London – although Kauffer never adopted British citizenship. Both paintings are dated 1915.
7. 'Montana artist upsets another British tradition', by R. Gram Swing, *Evening Post* (New York), 12 June 1926.
8. See Harvey L. Smith, *Mathews: Masterpieces of the California Decorative Style* (Oakland Museum, 1972) for an account of San Francisco art circles during Kauffer's period there.
9. The letter is with Mr Bernard Waldman, New York City.
10. Undated press cutting, Cooper-Hewitt Museum.
11. Records of the Art Institute of Chicago.
12. Article in *Portfolio*, op. cit.
13. Milton W. Brown, *The Story of the Armory Show* (New York, 1963), p. 178.
14. Article in *Portfolio*, op. cit.
15. Dated pastel of Venice by Kauffer in the collection of Mr S.A. Garrad, London; Maria Zimmern Petrie states in a letter to the author, 1970, that Kauffer attended an art school in Munich.
16. ed. Felix, Klee, *The Diaries of Paul Klee, 1898–1918* (London, 1965), p. 276.
17. *The Studio*, vol. LV, pp. 245–48.
18. *Art et Décoration*, vol. XXX, 1911, pp. 257–64.
19. Letter to the author, 1970.
20. Collection of Mr Brian Petrie, London; dated to spring 1914 by Maria Zimmern Petrie in a letter to the author, 1970.
21. Letter to the author, 1970.

Chapter 2: Painter into Designer

1. 'An Appreciation' by Sir Francis Meynell, E. McKnight Kauffer Memorial exhibition, Victoria and Albert Museum 1955.
2. 'E. McKnight Kauffer, Poster Designer', *Portfolio*, vol. 1, 1950, pp. 20–35.
3. 'Brief Biography' in exhibition catalogue of E. McKnight Kauffer posters at Museum of Modern Art, New York, 1937.
4. From Maria Zimmern Petrie's unpublished autobiography *Yesterday*. Collection of Brian Petrie, London.
5. Collection of Brian Petrie, London.
6. See n. 4.
7. Hassall's advice is recorded in Adolphe Armand Braun's article on Kauffer, *Commercial Art*, December 1923, pp. 324–6.
8. For a biography of Pick see Christian Barman, *The Man who made London Transport* (Newton Abbot, 1979). For a synoptic view of the posters see Michael F. Levey, *London Transport Posters* (London, 1976).
9. 'Architecture and Advertisements', an address to the Society of Arts on 1 December 1893 by Richardson Evans. *Journal of the Society of Arts*, vol. XLII, 1893, p. 39. Evans was secretary of SCAPA, and

eventually its historian: *An Account of the SCAPA Society* (London, 1926).
10. *A Beautiful World*, no. 5, December 1895: letter from Kipling accepting an invitation to join the Council of the Society for Checking the Abuses of Public Advertising.
11. *Fors Clavigera*, Letter 21 (September 1872). Ruskin refused to advertise his series of 'Letters to Working Men' and for many years prevented his publishers from even announcing his books in newspapers.
12. Michael Hiley, *Frank Meadow Sutcliffe* (London, 1974), p. 138. No particularly remarkable examples have come to light in Sutcliffe's surviving work.
13. Morris seconded a SCAPA resolution at the Society of Arts in January 1896. As might be expected, Morris's Socialist convictions gave him a wider view of the problem of advertising beyond the issue of urban and rural disfigurement. In 1893 he wrote to a fellow-member of SCAPA: 'I fear that there would be no slightest chance of success in attempting to tax (and thereby regulate) advertisements, except *in the streets*, where they are much less offensive than along the railways. You must remember that the advertisements you are speaking of are always on *private property*, and that in consequence it would be a revolutionary act to meddle with them. To tell you the plain truth, much as they annoy me personally, I cannot help rejoicing at the spectacle of the middle classes so annoyed and so helpless before the results of the idiotic tyranny which they themselves have created. . . .' (From a letter to Mrs E.J. Lowater, published in SCAPA's journal *A Beautiful World*, no. 10, September 1909, p. 94).
14. *A Beautiful World*, no. 10, September 1909, summarizing proposals made by Waterhouse much earlier in SCAPA's history and a consistent feature of SCAPA's programme from the beginning.
15. *Magazine of Art*, May 1881, vol. 18, p. 299.
16. E. McKnight Kauffer, *The Art of the Poster* (London, 1924), p. x.
17. Introduction to the International Exhibition of Posters at the Royal Aquarium, London 1894.
18. Charles T.J. Hiatt, *The Studio*, vol. 1, pp. 61–4. Perhaps a more obvious source of Hiatt's travesty is Ruskin's footnote 'The only living art now left in England is Bill-sticking', *Seven Lamps of Architecture* (Library edition, vol. 8), p. 194.
19. *The Studio*, vol. 23, 1901, pp. 51–2.
20. Ken Garland, 'The design of the London Underground diagram', *Penrose Annual*, vol. 62, 1969, pp. 68–82.
21. The posters referred to can be seen in the Department of Prints and Drawings of the Victoria and Albert Museum, as well as in the archives of London Transport. Of the poster by T.R. Way a good critic later wrote: 'The providential, if decidedly tardy, discovery of the "accidental" beauty of Lots Road Power Station in certain atmospheric conditions – the subject of one of the most famous of the earlier Underground posters which "the really artistic people" solemnly decided could be justified on the precedent of Whistler's nocturne study of Old Battersea Bridge – was an epoch-making event in the history of English commercial art'. P. Morton Shand, 'Underground', *Architectural Review*, November 1929, pp. 217–24.
22. Priscilla Johnston, *Edward Johnston* (London, 1959), p. 202.
23. *Architectural Review*, vol. 91, January 1942, pp. 1–2, an obituary of Frank Pick by Christian Barman.
24. E. McKnight Kauffer, 'Notes on Advertising Designing as a Career' in *Art Education Today* (New York, 1948), pp. 53–7.
25. See two exhibition catalogues published by the Fine Art Society, London: *The Earthly Paradise, F. Cayley Robinson and the painters of the Birmingham Group* (1969) and *Homage to Maxwell Armfield* (1970).
26. E. McKnight Kauffer, *The Art of the Poster*, p. x.

27. ed. R.W. Flint, *Marinetti: Selected Writings* (London, 1972), p. 67.
28. Guillaume Apollinaire, *Apollinaire on Art, Essays and Reviews 1902–1918* (London, 1972), p. 383.
29. Letter to the author, October 1970.
30. Kauffer's statement is from a pamphlet containing short personal texts by a number of designers, published under the title *The Art Preservative of all the Arts* by the Graphic Arts Production Yearbook, New York. A copy is in the Cooper-Hewitt Museum, New York.
31. The woodcut is often found, like other Kauffer woodcuts, dated 1922. However, this was merely the date when he made a series of impressions. The *Flight* woodcut was illustrated in *Apple* magazine, no. 1, 15 December 1919, p. 38.
32. Bevis Hillier unearthed this fascinating source and published in his *Art Déco of the 20s and 30s* (London, 1968), pp. 32–3, Suiseki's woodcut beside Kauffer's woodcut (which he identified in error as 'McKnight Kauffer's *Daily Herald* poster design of 1920'). The colour of the final poster reinforces the validity of Hillier's comparison. Kauffer may also have known Nikkwa's design of sparrows in flight from the *Khuhodo Gwafu* (1856), which is printed predominantly in black and beige. See L.G. Dawes, *Japanese Illustrated Books* (London, 1947), plate 47.
33. 'Brief Biography' – see n. 3.
34. The entire poster campaign, the posting of which was handled by S.H. Benson Ltd, was presented to the Victoria and Albert Museum by Ogilvy Benson and Mather Ltd in 1973. See V&A exhibition catalogue *Posters of a Lifetime* introduced by M. Haworth-Booth, London, 1973.
35. 'An Appreciation' – see n. 1.
36. Bevis Hillier was the first to notice the connection with Kauffer's *Flight* design, *Art Déco of the 20s and 30s*, p. 32.
37. Colin Hurry, 'An American Painter: E. McKnight Kauffer', *Pearson's Magazine*, June 1920.
38. Information from Mrs Peter Rendall.
39. Penguin Books edition (Harmondsworth, 1969, p. 641).
40. 'Brief Biography' – see no. 3.
41. Some designs were based on photographs taken in South America by William Zimmern (eg *Pompe Espina*). The original gouache designs were presented by him to the City of Manchester Art Gallery.
42. Coburn's photograph is in the International Museum of Photography at George Eastman House, Rochester, New York; Kauffer's oil painting is in the collection of Mrs Grevis Duce, Crediton.
43. A copy of the exhibition catalogue is in the Cooper-Hewitt Museum.
44. The Birmingham catalogue is also at the Cooper-Hewitt Museum.
45. Fry's letter, dated 5 April 1918, is in the Pierpont Morgan Library, New York (part of a group of letters, MA 1681). The letter is published in Denys Sutton, *Letters of Roger Fry*, vol. 2, pp. 426–7. The two volumes of letters contain other interesting details of the Fry-McKnight Kauffer friendship.
46. Letter to the author, 19 March 1974.
47. Kauffer had attempted to enlist in the British Army at the outbreak of war but had been rejected on grounds of citizenship; he was on his way to join the American Army when the war ended. Information from Mrs Peter Rendall.
48. Ana M. Berry, 'A Survey: Some younger artists and the A.L.S.', in *Design and Art* published by the ALS (London, 1928), p. 47. The article is a brief history of the ALS up to 1928 and it includes the puzzling remark (p. 53) that 'the first ALS dramatic tour in May, 1919, had been heralded (as have all subsequent tours) by a Kauffer poster'. At present only two are known – see checklist.
49. Catalogue of the exhibition held at the Mansard Gallery, 2–30 April 1921.

50. This and the following quotation are published in *Wyndham Lewis's Letters*, ed. W.K. Rose (London, 1963), pp. 112–15.
51. E. McKnight Kauffer, *The Art of the Poster*, p. x.
52. 'Brief Biography' – see n. 3.
53. Wyndham Lewis, *Blasting and Bombardiering* (London, 1937), p. 211.

Chapter 3: The Early Twenties

1. A.M. Cassandre, introduction to *Art International d'aujourd'hui no. 12: Publicité* (Paris, 1929): 'L'affiche n'est plus un tableau mais devient une "machine à annoncer". Le catalogue, l'annonce, l'enseigne lumineuse, autant d'objets vivants qui font aujourd'hui partie de notre vie quotidienne comme le téléphone et la machine à écrire'. The statement is not quoted in full here but shows how close Kauffer was to Parisian artists working in publicity. For Cassandre, 'Toute une génération d'artistes trouve en lui [publicité] son mode d'expression le plus vivant'.
2. The Evansville Museum of Arts and Sciences holds an extensive collection of these.
3. 'E. McKnight Kauffer, Poster Designer', *Portfolio*, vol. 1, 1950, pp. 30–35.
4. Penguin Books edition (Harmondsworth, 1951), p. 27.
5. Reproduced in *Evelyn Waugh and His World*, ed. David Pryce-Jones (London, 1973).
6. A useful contemporary account is Frank Sidgwick, 'The Westminster Press – its history and its activities', *The Studio*, vol. 99, 1930, p. 438. Priscilla Johnston characterized Gerard Meynell as 'small and dark with a hooked nose, a blue chin and flashing spectacles. He resembled the popular idea of a newspaper man, cocking his head like a sparrow, his hat pushed back and – almost – his thumbs hooked into his waistcoat': *Edward Johnston* (London, 1959), p. 191. For Meynell's taste as a typographer see his *Pages from Books* (Lanston Monotype Corporation, 1927).
7. Kauffer kept a copy of this all his life and it is now in the Cooper-Hewitt Museum, New York.
8. *Commercial Art*, November 1923, p. 320.
9. *The London Mercury*, October 1921, p. 16.
10. *Commercial Art*, December 1923, pp. 322–3, 327–8 records the debate.
11. *Penrose Annual*, 1924.
12. The company's appreciative letter is in the Cooper-Hewitt Museum.
13. *The Times*, 18 May 1927.
14. Tributes to Grace McKnight Kauffer have been preserved in a *Memorial of Grace McKnight*, privately printed by Peter and Ann Rendall, Bembridge, Isle of Wight, 1966.
15. Wyndham Lewis, *Blasting and Bombardiering* (London, 1937), p. 211.
16. *Commercial Art*, October 1923, pp. 274–5.
17. Ibid.
18. See *The Chap-Book: A Miscellany* (London, 1924) for the illustration to Eliot and the portrait of Monro. The original drawing for the latter is now in the Poetry Collection of the Lockwood Memorial Library, State University of New York, Buffalo.
19. On an objection from the landlord the sign was placed flat against the front wall of the shop (rather than at right-angles); this explains the excellent state of preservation of one side of the board and the severe blistering of the other. A photograph of Monro with the board is reproduced in Robert H. Ross, *The Georgian Revolt: Rise and Fall of a Poetic Ideal 1910–22* (London, 1967), opposite p. 96.
20. See Eleanor Elder, *Travelling Players: the story of the A.L.S.* (London, 1939), in which a plate reproduces Kauffer's costumes for Anatole France's *The Man Who Married a Dumb Wife* (1923–4). Kauffer also designed a screen for Chekhov's *The Proposal* (1925–6), costumes for *Henry VIII* (1925–6) and symbols for *Lazarus*, presumably about the same date.
21. Two of the originals are at London Transport and are titled Whitsuntide rather than Summertime, and the set is often confusingly reproduced or referred to as illustrating Whitsuntide. However, sets of the printed posters are lettered for both Whitsuntide and Summer – presumably they were issued twice. The reasons for this are not known.
22. Catalogue of Kauffer's retrospective exhibition, Arts League of Service London, 1925.

23. See n. 20.
24. *Vogue*, early August 1925, p. 54.
25. Sir Francis Meynell, 'An Appreciation', E. McKnight Kauffer Memorial exhibition, Victoria and Albert Museum 1955.
26. As above.
27. Colour plate from an unidentified magazine, dated June 1926, in Kauffer's guardbooks, Victoria and Albert Museum.
28. The dress has a zig-zag pattern at the sleeves and a hem decorated with stylized roses and thistles. It is in the collection of Mrs Rosemary Pepler, Ditchling.
29. See n. 25. Meynell's side of the correspondence has now come to light in the Pierpont Morgan Library, New York, and will be treated in a forthcoming study of the Nonesuch Press by John Dreyfus and Simon Rendall.
30. This and the following remarks are from Fry's essay 'The Author and the Artist', first published in the *Burlington Magazine*, July 1926, pp. 9–12, and collected by Fry in his *Transformations, Critical and speculative essays on art* (London, 1926).
31. A typescript of notes taken at the lecture, perhaps by Kauffer himself, differs significantly from the pamphlet. It is preserved in the Pierpont Morgan Library, New York.
32. *Spectator*, 17 March 1923.

Chapter 4: The Late Twenties

1. Letter to the author, 17 January 1972.
2. Harold Acton, *Memoirs of an Aesthete* (London, 1948), p. 198.
3. *The Times*, 13 September 1958. A.L.F. Smith paid a splendid personal tribute to Tallents in the issue of 17 September, including praise for Tallents's 'brilliant nervous prose which he wrote down with a sliver of a pen which he must have used for 50 years'.
4. Gervas Huxley, *Both Hands* (London, 1970). Chapter 6 is the best inside account of the E.M.B. yet in print. The quotation is from p. 126.
5. From Tallents's unpublished book on the E.M.B., *Empire Experiment*, which his son Mr T.W. Tallents kindly allowed me to see.
6. Quoted by Tallents in his article 'The Birth of British Documentary', *Journal of the University Film Association*, vol. 20, nos. 1–3.
7. Tallents, 'The Birth of British Documentary', 1, op.cit.
8. Tallents, *The Projection of England*, 2nd edition (London, 1955), p. 34. His official report on the Barcelona exhibition is Public Record Office E.M.B./P.C./135.
9. Letter to the author, 7 July 1972.
10. Mildred Constantine and Alan M. Fern, *Word and Image, Posters from the collection of the Museum of Modern Art* (New York, 1968), repr. p. 77 (original design in tempera).
11. Cooper-Hewitt Museum records.
12. Letter to the author, 1 August 1973. For Ivor Montagu Kauffer also designed an international badge for the English Table Tennis Association – 'a Kauffer version of the English rose – very good indeed – which so surprised and bewildered the players – it was ahead of the taste of the time – that two at least sewed it on their blazers upside down'. Mr Montagu kindly presented an example to the Textiles Department of the V&A.
13. The only known copy is in the Museum of Modern Art, New York.
14. See n. 5.
15. *Advertiser's Weekly*, 10.12.26.
16. Public Record Office, E.M.B. papers: CO.760.3. EMB/PC/93 (10.12.28) – Report on the efficacy of the Board's Poster Publicity.
17. Public Record Office, E.M.B. papers: CO.760.22. Publicity Committee Papers 2, paragraph 5.
18. See Tallents, *Empire Experiment*, op cit., for details of the poster campaign.
19. The original design is in the Victoria and Albert Museum: as it was used at bulletin-board, or 16 sheet, size Kauffer was paid 100 guineas for it. For his 'National Mark' design he received 35 guineas. Public Record Office, E.M.B./PC/Poster subcommittee papers 21.7.27 and 19.4.28. In general fees were £75 for a poster, £15 for a showcard – 29.9.27.
20. Conversation, 12 January 1971.
21. *Empire Experiment*, op. cit., p. 43.

22. Ashley recorded how Stanley Morison introduced him to Kauffer's work in his Prologue to Michael Frostick, *Advertising and the Motor Car* (London, 1970), p. 12: 'Morison's advice to me on this occasion was: get out of advertising and find something worth while to do – or, alternatively, *do something constructive to improve the dreadful appearance of advertising* (this is 1923) which was still reflecting the visual vulgarity of the late nineteenth-century printing and advertising with its crude illustrations, ugly display typefaces and even worse body types for the setting of text matter. Morison continued by observing that if I must work in advertising, I should try to do something like this – and at that point he handed me a small printed showcard he had on his desk for "Eastmans" (the dry cleaners). This depicted a very "cubist" sort of design in bright colours signed by an artist entirely strange to me: "E Mc K K". Morison went on to say that if I didn't like this, then I ought to get to like it, because it was an example of what the modern poster was going to be.'
23. Conversations with Ashley and Mr Hellicar, 1972.
24. Stenberg's poster is reproduced in the University of Texas Art Museum exhibition catalogue *Russian Painters and the Stage 1884–1965* (1978), plate 99.
25. *Gebrauchsgraphic*, May 1929, p. 45.
26. Dr Desmond Flower, 'The Book Illustrations of E. McKnight Kauffer', *Penrose Annual*, London, 1956, pp. 35–40.
27. Ibid.
28. Letter from Eliot to Kauffer, 24 July 1930, carbon copy in collection of Mrs Valerie Eliot.
29. Roger Fry congratulated Kauffer on precisely this quality in a letter on the Robinson Crusoe illustrations: 'I trembled for you when I saw the title but once more you've found the way by a miracle of tact and sensibility. Its amazing to me how you manage never to block any of the avenues of the reader's imagination by any too precise image: how you manage by the subtlest allusions to show how much you have understood and how carefully you have refrained from imposing that on us. The images are all like Japanese stop-shorts, where the words stop but the sense goes on.' Unpublished letter dated 27 November 1929, Pierpont Morgan Library, New York (MA 1681).
30. Letter from Kauffer to Eliot, 15 September 1927, in the collection of Mrs Valerie Eliot.
31. Letter from Eliot to Kauffer, Pierpont Morgan Library, New York (no. MA 1667).
32. Letter from Kauffer to Eliot dated 10 October 1929, in the collection of Mrs Valerie Eliot.
33. Letter from Kauffer to Eliot dated 29 July 1930 in collection of Mrs Valerie Eliot.
34. Letter from Eliot to Kauffer dated 8 August 1930, Pierpont Morgan Library, New York (no. MA 1667). This version of the design is in the Cooper-Hewitt Museum; an earlier version is in the collection of Lord Hutchinson Q.C., London.
35. Leonard Woolf, *Downhill All the Way* (London, 1967).
36. Collection of Mrs Valerie Eliot.
37. Letter from Eliot to Kauffer dated 15 December 1929, Pierpont Morgan Library (no. MA 1667).
38. Undated letter, source as above.
39. Letter from Eliot to Kauffer, 30 May 1949, including a 'profile' of Kauffer written at the artist's request: carbon copy in collection of Mrs Valerie Eliot.
40. Notes by T.S. Eliot for the Memorial Exhibition of Kauffer's work at the V&A, opened on 6 October 1955. Eliot's address was given by tape-recording as he himself was indisposed, due to a foot infection. The notes are in the collection of Mrs Valerie Eliot.
41. See *The Studio*, January 1929, pp. 35–9. See also Valerie Mendes, 'Marion Dorn, Textile Designer', *Bulletin of the Decorative Arts Society 1890–1940*, no. 2, 1978, pp. 24–35. Also the exhibition catalogue introduced by Jacqueline Pruskin, *British Carpets and Designs: the Modernist Rug 1928–1938*, Royal Pavilion, Art Gallery and Museums, Brighton 1975.
42. The rug was item H12 in the exhibition catalogue *Victorian and Edwardian Decorative Art: The Handley-Read Collection*, Royal Academy of Arts 1972 (pp. 130–31), and was later generously presented to the V&A by Lady Ashton.
43. Letter from Bennett to Kauffer, Pierpont Morgan Library, New York (no. MA 1664).
44. See *Architectural Review*, July 1931 for the only surviving photographic record.

45. Letter from Bennett to Kauffer dated 18.9.1930, Pierpont Morgan Library, New York (no. MA 1664).
46. 'E. McKnight Kauffer, Poster Designer', *Portfolio*, vol. 1, 1950, pp. 20–35.

Chapter 5: The Thirties (1)

1. Osbert Sitwell, *Noble Essences* (London, 1950). p. 304.
2. 'The Book Illustrations of E. McKnight Kauffer', *Penrose Annual*, London, 1956, pp. 35–40. Dr Flower himself owns two of the abandoned designs.
3. Recollections of Jeanette Rutherston Powell in conversation with the author, 1971. The Nicholson relief, of 1938, is reproduced in *Ben Nicholson: paintings, reliefs, drawings* (London, 1948), plate 71.
4. Recollections of the late Freddie Mayor in conversation with the author, 1971. The Baumeister, whereabouts now unknown, was acquired in 1931–2.
5. Recollections of Lord Clark in conversation with the author, 1971.
6. *Advertising Review*, vol. 1, no. 3, Winter 1954–5. p. 36.
7. See n. 5.
8. Letters to the author, July–August 1970.
9. Examples are in the Department of Prints, Drawings and Photographs at the V&A.
10. Recollections of Mrs Peter Rendall in conversation with the author, 1970.
11. Illustrated in the *Architectural Review*, June 1933, p. 261.
12. *Architectural Review*, August 1937, p. 51.
13. The building and the photo-mural were featured in *Architectural Review*, vol. XXXIII, 1935, pp. 167–73. Details of the process were provided by Mr Eugene Mollo in conversation in 1979. The photo-mural at Embassy Court no longer exists.
14. Kauffer's statement was published in an *Architectural Review* 'Decoration' supplement on the photo-mural technique in February 1937, together with 14 illustrations; two of these show the photo-mural on Earl's Court referred to below.
15. The space-frame may derive from Herbert Bayer, whose poster for the German section at the Exposition de la société des artistes décorateurs, Grand Palais, Paris 1934 certainly contains ideas which Kauffer used in 1937 (*Lubrication by Shell, Miles-Whitney Straight aeroplane*) – see *Herbert Bayer: painter, designer, architect* (London and New York, 1967), p. 31. The painted clouds often used by Kauffer in the later thirties probably come from Bayer also – see the Cinzano poster (1934) in the Bayer monograph, p. 47. On the other hand Kauffer's Embassy Court photo-mural may well have influenced Moholy-Nagy's brilliant layout, 'Leisure at the Seaside', for the *Architectural Review* in July 1936.
16. *The Times*, 12 February 1959. The obituary was published on the previous day; further tributes included contributions from Jane B. Drew (14 February) Henry Moore (19 February).
17. Sir Herbert E. Read and Sir Charles Morris, *Eric Craven Gregory* (the addresses in tribute at The Cathedral, Bradford, on Monday 2 March 1959 by Sir Charles Morris and at St Lukes Church, Chelsea, on Thursday 5 March 1959 by Sir Herbert Read) London, 1959. See also the catalogue of the Gregory Memorial Exhibition, Leeds City Art Gallery, 1960, introduced by Herbert Read: 'his long and intimate association with E. McKnight Kauffer should not be forgotten. Kauffer is chiefly remembered as a poster artist, but he was a sensitive and extremely intelligent man whose talent was applied in many directions' (p. 5). For further information on Gregory's collection, see Sotheby's sale catalogues for 4 November 1959 (paintings and sculpture), 26 October 1959 (books), 11 February 1960 (lithographs and other prints). The first sale included a Kauffer oil, *Easel and Chair* 1939, present whereabouts unknown.
18. The gallery is described and illustrated in Dorothy Todd, 'Marion Dorn, Architect of Floors', *Architectural Review*, October 1933.
19. See James L. Enyeart, *Bruguière: His Photographs and his Life* (New York, 1977), pp. 93–4, and plate 67.
20. Conversation with Man Ray, Paris, March 1970.
21. Reproduced in a cutting from an unknown publication, Cooper-Hewitt Museum, New York.
22. *Guardian*, 15 March 1935.

23. *Spectator*, 5 April 1935.
24. Notes for BBC/TV talk on Kauffer, The Library, King's College, Cambridge, 1955.
25. Conversation with Lord Clark, 1970.
26. *Advertising Review*, vol. 1, no. 3, Winter 1954–5, p. 35.
27. The most valuable existing contribution is Valerie Mendes, 'Marion Dorn, Textile Designer', *Bulletin of the Decorative Arts Society 1890–1940*, no. 2, 1978, pp. 24–35. This deals with Marion Dorn's work in England.
28. Conversation with Lady Robinson, January 1973.
29. Sir Colin Anderson, 'Ship interiors – when the breakthrough came', *Architectural Review*, June 1967, pp. 449–52.
30. Reproduced in *Architectural Review*, October 1935, p. 157.
31. *Trend*, Spring 1936.
32. Ibid.
33. Tallents, *Empire Experiment*, op. cit.
34. Herbert Read, 'Novelism at the R A', *Architectural Review*, February 1935.

Chapter 6: The Thirties (2)

1. Conversation with Lord Clark, 1971. Beddington's career is described in an obituary in *The Times* for 15 April 1959; tributes were subsequently published on 16 April (Nicholas Bentley), 17 April (C.M. Vignoles and Bryan Robertson), 22 April (Paul Rotha), 27 April (John Betjeman). I am grateful to Colonel Freddie Beddington for supplying other details.
2. *In Fifty Years of Shell Advertising*, brochure of an exhibition held at 195 Piccadilly in 1969.
3. *The Times*, 17 April 1959.
4. The Kauffer paintings owned by Beddington were: *View at Cassis* (1935) and *Cornfield with Stooks and Distant Cottage*, lots 64 and 141 respectively in the sale of most of Beddington's collection, Christie's, 25 March 1960.
5. Collection of Mrs Christopher Lobb, Penzance, Cornwall.
6. Letter dated 17.11.29, collection of Mrs Lobb, as are the other letters from Kauffer to Beddington quoted by her kind permission in this chapter and the next.
7. A copy is in the Osborne Robinson collection, Northampton College of Art.
8. 24 November 1935.
9. 12 May 1936.
10. 21 May 1936.
11. Collection of Whitney Straight, Esq. London.
12. *Architectural Review*, December 1929, p. 276 shows a country garage before, during and after the removal of advertising signs.
13. E. McKnight Kauffer, 'The Designer and the Public', *Journal of the Royal Society of Arts*, vol. 87, 1938, pp. 51 ff.
14. Ibid.
15. Kenneth Clark, Preface to Roger Fry's *Last Lectures* (Cambridge 1939), p. vi: '. . . we have seen a series of events so tragic and horrible that our indignation can hardly fail to overflow and swamp out detached contemplation of shapes and colours. To be a pure painter seems almost immoral.'
16. See n. 13.
17. *Morning Post*, 5 April 1932.
18. *Observer*, 10 April 1932.
19. A number of set and costume designs are preserved in the Cooper-Hewitt Museum, New York, and in the collection of Dr Richard Wunder, Orwell, Vermont.
20. *Morning Post*, 9 June 1934.
21. *Sunday Times*, 8 June 1934.
22. Clive Barnes, 'Checkmate', *Dance and Dancers*, February 1963, pp. 31–3.
23. P.W. Manchester, *Vic-Wells: A Ballet Progress* (London, 1942), p. 38.
24. Details of the ballet can be added from Ninette de Valois, *Come Dance With Me: A Memoir* (London, 1957), p. 119 and Mary Clarke, *The Sadler's Wells Ballet* (London, 1955), p. 133.
25. Conversation with Irene Wellington, 1972 (also the source of the following remarks about the White House).
26. Letters in the collection of Mrs Peter Rendall, quoted with her kind permission.
27. Pierpont Morgan Library, New York (MA 1667).
28. Collection of Mrs Valerie Eliot.
29. See n. 27.
30. See n. 27.

31. Peter Gregory's diary (1940–41) entry for 15 July. Collection of Jane B. Drew, London, and quoted with her kind permission.
32. Ministry of Information records: INFI/33 Staff organization General Production Division – 13/5/40 O.E.P.E.C.
33. *Advertising Review*, vol. 1, no. 3, Winter 1954–5, p. 33.

Chapter 7: New York, 1940–54

1. By kind permission of Mrs Christopher Lobb.
2. By kind permission of Sir Colin Anderson KBE
3. Pierpont Morgan Library, New York (MA 1667).
4. Collection of Mrs Valerie Eliot.
5. Lady Ashton – conversation 1970.
6. *Advertising Art Now* by E. McKnight Kauffer, from an address given before the Art Directors Club, New York 1941. (16 pp. with illustration of *Flight* on cover.) Cooper-Hewitt Museum, New York.
7. Introduction to Paul Rand, *Thoughts on Design* (New York, 1947).
8. J.I. Biegeleisen, *Poster Design* (New York, 1945), p. 1.
9. T.S. Eliot, notes for the opening of Kauffer's memorial exhibition at the Victoria and Albert Museum, October 1955 (Mrs Valerie Eliot).
10. He liked to visit Harlem's night-spots with young English friends like Jeremy Hutchinson (now Lord Hutchinson). He also illustrated Carl Van Vechten's unpublished book *Nigger Heaven* and his original water-colours for this are preserved in the Museum of Modern Art, New York.
11. Speech printed on single sheet, author's collection.
12. D. Flower, 'The Book Illustrations of E. McKnight Kauffer', *Penrose Annual*, London, 1956, pp. 35–40.
13. See Beeleigh Abbey Books, catalogue 12, pt. 1, 663: includes Kauffer letter to Eliot of November 1929 on this subject.
14. Letter to the author, 21 November 1973.
15. *Dance and Dancers* for December '54 (p. 23) states that Kauffer revised his designs 'to fit in with de Valois' insistence on a more stylised less human interpretation of the leading roles', but Dame Ninette (letter to the author, March 1979) confirms that the slight changes made were all of Kauffer's choosing, and she regretted most the simplification of the double-bass shaped Red Bishops' costumes: 'the originals were wonderful – but cumbersome and difficult to travel, hence, no doubt, the change'.
16. Preserved by Grace Schulman, who has very generously allowed me to quote the Marianne Moore texts in her possession.
17. Letter from Grace Schulman to Mrs Peter Rendall, 1974.
18. E. McKnight Kauffer, 'The Poster – What it is and why', *Travel USA*, April 1949.
19. *Portfolio*, vol. 1, 1950, pp. 20–35.
20. Letter from Eliot to Kauffer, 30 May 1949 – carbon copy in collection of Mrs Valerie Eliot.
21. Man Ray, *Self Portrait* (London, 1963), p. 323.
22. Sir Francis Meynell, 'An Appreciation', McKnight Kauffer Memorial exhibition catalogue, Victoria and Albert Museum 1955: 'Kauffer was a warm and generous man, but came to suffer from the delusion that his friends despised him for having returned to the USA early in the war. What nonsense! It was the only sensible thing for him to do. But no reassurance could prevail, and he insisted on his own sense of guilt which nobody shared; and this made him aloof from many who loved him, and wished him close and well.'
23. See n. 19.
24. Kauffer to Beddington, 31 October 1950 (Mrs Christopher Lobb).
25. Kauffer to Barman, 26 July 1950 (Christian Barman, Esq).
26. See n. 6.
27. Cooper-Hewitt Museum, New York.
28. Marion Dorn bequeathed a collection of some 1100 items of work and memorabilia of Kauffer's to the Cooper-Hewitt Museum, and collections of his posters were given to the Rochester Institute of Technology, New York, and to the American Museum at Bath in England. She died in Tangiers in 1964.
29. Eliot to Marion Dorn, 7 November 1954 (carbon copy with Mrs Valerie Eliot).
30. Eliot's notes for opening address, Kauffer memorial exhibition at Victoria and Albert Museum, October 1955 (Mrs Valerie Eliot).
31. Marianne Moore to Eliot, 27 October 1954 (Mrs Valerie Eliot).

Select Bibliography

Note: Kauffer's own press-cuttings books are preserved at the
Cooper-Hewitt Museum, New York City, and a file of cuttings
is also held by the Evansville Museum of Arts and Science,
Indiana.
Further references are given in the acknowledgements,
footnotes to text and checklist.

Exhibition Catalogues (one-man)

Paintings by E. McKnight Kauffer, Hampshire House,
Hammersmith, London, 1916. Foreword by Alvin Langdon
Coburn
Posters by E. McKnight Kauffer, Arts League of Service Galleries,
London, 1925, and the Ashmolean Museum, Oxford, 1926.
Foreword and notes by Roger Fry
Watercolour drawings by E. McKnight Kauffer, Arthur Tooth and
Sons Gallery, London, 1933
The Work of E. McKnight Kauffer, Lund Humphries & Co Gallery,
London, 1935
Posters by E. McKnight Kauffer, Museum of Modern Art, New
York, 1937. Foreword by Aldous Huxley. Note on Technique
by McKnight Kauffer
*Drawings for the ballet and original illustrations for Edgar Allan
Poe*, American–British Art Gallery, Batsford House, New
York, 1949. Foreword by Marianne Moore
Memorial Exhibition of the work of E. McKnight Kauffer, Victoria
and Albert Museum, London, 1955. Opened by T.S. Eliot, OM.
Introduction by Ashley Havinden. Appreciation by Sir
Francis Meynell. Note by Thomas Eckersley
Posters by E. McKnight Kauffer, IBM gallery, New York, 1969.
Introduction by Paul Rand
E. McKnight Kauffer. Poster Art 1915–1940, Travelling
exhibition arranged by the Circulation Department of the
Victoria and Albert Museum, London, 1973. Text by Mark
Haworth-Booth

Exhibition catalogues (group)

The London Group, London, 1916–19
*Paintings and Drawings by E. McKnight Kauffer and Barry V.
Jackson*, Birmingham Repertory Theatre, 1917. Introduction
by Roger Fry. Also shown as part of The New Movement in
Art, selected by Fry, at the Mansard Gallery, London, later in
the same year
Group X, Mansard Gallery, 1920. Foreword by Wyndham Lewis
Groupe de Peintres Modernes, Galerie Druet, Paris, 1921
The Friday Club, Mansard Gallery, London, 1921
Present day industrial art, Victoria and Albert Museum, 1922
Mostra Internazionale delle Arti Decorativi, Milan, 1923
British Industrial Art for the Slender Purse, Victoria and Albert
Museum, 1929
Modern Pictorial Advertising by Shell, New Burlington Galleries,
London, 1931. Foreword by Robert Byron: 'Responsible
Publicity'
British Industrial Art in relation to the home, Dorland Hall,
London, 1933
Pictures in advertising 1935–38, Royal Watercolour Society
Galleries, London, 1938
The Advance Guard of Advertising Artists, Katharine Kuh Gallery,
Chicago, 1941 and then A–D Gallery, New York, 1942
Posters of a Lifetime, Bethnal Green Museum, 1973.
Introduction by Mark Haworth-Booth
Artists at Curwen, Tate Gallery, London, 1977. Catalogue by
Pat Gilmour

Teaspoons to Trains: the work of Frank Pick, 1878–1941, Victoria
and Albert Museum, 1978 (arranged by Barbara Morris,
Jennifer Hawkins and Geoffrey Opie)
Thirties: British art and design before the war, Arts Council of
Great Britain and Victoria and Albert Museum, 1979

Statements by Kauffer

'The Poster', *Arts and Decoration*, New York, November 1921
'The essentials of poster design', *Arts League of Service Bulletin
1923–24*, London, 1924
'The Poster and symbolism', *Penrose Annual*, London, 1924
The Art of the Poster, London, 1924. Note: 100 copies of the
book containing a poster by Kauffer were issued in addition
to the ordinary edition
'When I design a poster . . .', *Daily Review*, London, 19 July
1933
'The Photomural', *Architectural Review*, London, February
1937
'Art and advertising, the designer and the public', *Journal of the
Royal Society of Arts*, vol. 87, pp. 51–70, London, 1938
Advertising art now. An address to the Art Directors' Club of
New York, New York, 1941
Foreword to *Thoughts on Design* by Paul Rand, New York, 1947

Statements about Kauffer

C. Hurry, 'An American painter: E. McKnight Kauffer',
Pearson's Magazine, June 1920
H. Taylor, 'The poster revival no. 1 – E. McKnight Kauffer', *The
Studio* vol. 79, 1920, pp. 140–47
R.A. Parker, 'A commercial artist with ideals', *Arts and
Decoration*, New York, November 1921
H.K. Willoughby, 'Modernism in poster art', *The Poster*, May
1923
A.A. Braun, 'Artists who help the advertiser – E. McKnight
Kauffer', *Commercial Art*, December 1923, pp. 324–6
Raymond Mortimer (article unsigned), 'The Posters of
E. McKnight Kauffer', *Vogue*, Late May 1925
R. Gram Swing, 'Montana artist upsets another British
tradition', *Evening Post*, New York, 12 June 1926
R. Fry, 'The author and the artist', *Transformations*, London,
1926
G.S. Sandilands, 'E. McKnight Kauffer', *Commercial Art*, July
1927
W.G. Archer, 'E. McKnight Kauffer and T.S. Eliot', *Cambridge
Review*, 1 May 1931
G. Grigson, 'The Evolution of E. McKnight Kauffer, a Master
Designer', *Commercial Art* vol. XVIII, 1935, pp. 202–6
A. Blunt, *Spectator*, 5 April 1935, p. 567
Anonymous, 'E. McKnight Kauffer: poster designer', *Portfolio*
vol. 1, Cincinnati, 1950, pp. 20–35
H. Schleger, Sir F. Meynell, J. Beddington, C. Barman,
E.C. Gregory, A. Havinden and Sir C. Anderson, 'E. McKnight
Kauffer, a memorial symposium', *Advertising Review* vol. 1,
no. 3, Winter 1954–5
C. Rosner, 'In Memoriam: E. McKnight Kauffer', *Graphis* vol.
11, 1955, p. 10
D. Flower, 'Book illustrations by E. McKnight Kauffer', *Penrose
Annual*, 1956
K. Murgatroyd, 'E. McKnight Kauffer: the artist in commerce',
Print, New York, January 1969
M. Haworth-Booth, 'E. McKnight Kauffer', *Penrose Annual*,
1971

Checklist of published works

A checklist compiled by Mark Haworth-Booth and Alan Howell

This checklist is abstracted from a comprehensive listing of Kauffer's work in all design fields, a typescript of which will be lodged by the compilers in the Library of the Victoria and Albert Museum. Posters exclude 'car-panels' and 'show-cards'.

Each entry is arranged as follows:
Category of work. Title or short description.
Client. Collection or reference.

Title

As printed on the item, or a short description where no title is applicable. In the case of book jackets and theatrical works this is followed by the name of the author.

Category of work

P	Poster	Bi	Book illustration
Lb	Lorry bill	Bj	Book jacket

Client

Clients are represented in the checklist by a keyword or initials. The following is a list of those principally used:

ALS	Arts League of Service, London
ARP	Air Raid Precautions, London
BEE	British Empire Exhibition, Wembley, 1924
Bass	Bass Ltd, brewers, London
C + W	Chatto & Windus, publishers, London
CWM	Canadian War Memorials
Constable	Constable and Co Ltd, publishers, London
D + T	Derry & Toms Ltd, department store, High St Kensington, London
Eastman	Eastman & Sons Ltd, Acton, London
Empire	The Empire Marketing Board, London
Eno	J.C. Eno Ltd
GPO	General Post Office, London
GWR	Great Western Railways
Gollancz	Victor Gollancz Ltd, publishers, London
Heals	Heal & Son Ltd, Tottenham Court Road, London
Heinemann	Heinemann Ltd, publishers, London
Hutchinson	Hutchinson Ltd, publishers, London
Imperial	Imperial Airways
LG	London Group
LPTB	London Passenger Transport Board
LT	London Transport
L + V Woolf	L & V Woolf Ltd, publishers, London
MG	*Manchester Guardian*
Modern Library	Modern Library (Random House) publishers, New York

Nonesuch	Nonesuch Press, London
Orient	Orient Line, Anderson Green & Co Ltd, London
Pan Am	Pan American Airways
Pomeroy	Pomeroy, manufacturers of Day Cream Interamericanos Washington EUA
Publicado	Publicado por E C Coordinador de Asontos
Putnam	Putnam & Co Ltd, publishers, London
Ringling	Ringling Brothers, Barnum & Bailey, Circus
Shell	Shell-Mex Ltd, London
SMAC	Spanish Medical Aid Committee
UCSSA	United Committee of South Slavic Americans
UD	The Underground Railways Co of London Ltd
Villiers	Villiers Motor Cycle Co Ltd
Vogue	*Vogue* magazine, London
WAG	W & A Gilbey Ltd, wines & spirits
WB	Walker Bros
Wolseley	Wolseley Cars
WP	Westminster Press

Source of Information

A guide to where a printed example or reference can be found. Sources are abbreviated as follows:

AMB	American Museum in Britain, Bath
CHM	Cooper-Hewitt Museum of Decorative Art and Design
HH	Hampshire House, exhibition catalogue, Hammersmith 1916
IWM	Imperial War Museum, London
LoC	Library of Congress, Washington DC
MMA	Museum of Modern Art, New York
SG	Sidney Garrad Collection, London
V&A	Victoria and Albert Museum, London
(od)	indicates original design

Sizes

The principal sizes used by Kauffer's clients for posters were as follows:

London Transport
DC (Double Crown)	30″ × 20″	76.2 × 50.8cm
DR (Double Royal)	40″ × 25″	101.6 × 63.5cm

Shell-Mex
2 sheet lorrybill	30″ × 40″	76.2 × 101.6cm

American Airlines
QC (Quad-Crown)	40″ × 30″	101.6 × 76.2cm

Pan American
QC (Quad-Crown)	40″ × 30″	101.6 × 76.2cm

Some posters were also produced in larger sizes, for example, The Early Bird 1919, 12 sheet; Horse Power, 1933, 48 sheet. Some posters were produced as handbills, for example American Airlines, Niagara Falls and Canada 1948, 22 × 16.5cm

1915

In Watford
P/UD/V&A, LoC, V&A (od)
Oxhey Woods
P/UD/V&A, MMA, CHM, LoC
Reigate
P/UD/V&A, LoC, V&A (od)
The Heaths, Surrey
P/UD/V&A, LoC
note: listed in HH as Beyond Esher
Godstone
P/UD/V&A, CHM, LoC
The North Downs
P/UD/V&A, LoC, V&A (od)
Shere
P/UD
Listed in HH no 7, no printed example known

1917

Derry and Toms, Economy and Smartness in men's wear
P/D&T/V&A, MMA
Autumn Offerings
P/D&T/MMA exhib cat no 1
Vigil the pure silk
P/od exhib at Wyndham Lewis exhib, TG 1956

1918

Canadian War Memorials Exhibition
P/CWM/IWM
The London Group
P/LG/MMA

1919

The Early Bird, Soaring to success – the *Daily Herald*
P/*Daily Herald*/V&A, MMA (top only)
Summer Sale at Derry and Toms
P/D&T/V&A, MMA, LoC
Winter Sale at Derry and Toms
P/D&T/V&A, MMA
Objects from the East at Derry and Toms
P/D&T/SG
Modern Art
P/LG/coll Mr & Mrs P. Rendall, Burford, CHM
Vigil the pure silk
P/WB/CHM, MMA, SG (od)
The Golden Ballot
P/ALS exhib cat 1925, no printed example known
Arts League of Service
P/ALS/coll M.B. Zimmern, London

1920

Uxbridge by Tram
P/Tram/V&A, LoC, V&A (od)
Hatfield by Motor Bus
P/Omnibus/V&A
Reigate-Priory Park by Motor Bus
P/Omnibus/V&A
Hainault Forest by Motor Bus
P/Omnibus/V&A
St Albans by Motor Bus
P/Omnibus/V&A, V&A (od)
note: the V&A also hold ten sheets showing stage proofs
   of this six-colour design
Windsor by Motor Bus
P/Omnibus/V&A, LoC
Chingford by Motor Bus
P/Omnibus/V&A, LoC
The Forest Glades of Epping
P/Omnibus/V&A
Epping Forest by Motor Bus
P/Omnibus/V&A, LoC, V&A (od)
Aster Time, Kew Gardens
P/UD/V&A
Flowers of the hills . . . on the Surrey Uplands
P/UD/V&A, LoC
Flowers o' the corn
P/UD/V&A, LoC, V&A (od)
Bluebells, Kew Gardens
P/UD/coll Mr & Mrs P. Rendall, Burford
Flowers of the Riverside
P/UD/SG, LoC
Group X
P/Group X/SG, MMA

1921

Victoria and Albert Museum
P/UD/CHM, MMA
London Museum of Practical Geology
P/UD/V&A, MMA
British Museum – Yemma Tem
P/UD/SG (od)
Chislehurst by Motor Bus
P/Omnibus/SG
Shop between 10 & 4. The quiet hours
P/UD/MMA, SG
Winter Sales are best reached by Underground
P/UD/V&A, MMA, V&A (od)
Eastman's Tailor Valet Service
P/Eastman/SG
London Dyers and Cleaners for over 100 years (magic
   dyers)
P/Eastman/V&A
Vigil the pure silk – for lovely frocks
P/WB/SG
Eminent Victorians by Lytton Strachey
Bj/C&W/SG

1922

Winter Sales are best reached by Underground
P/UD/V&A, MMA
The Royal United Services Museum
P/UD/V&A
The Rocket of Mr Stephenson of Newcastle 1829,
   Museum of Science
P/UD/V&A, MMA, V&A (od)
London History at The London Museum
P/UD/V&A, MMA, V&A (od)
note: reprinted by LT in 1966
Gloves cleaned, colour and beauty restored
P/Eastman/SG
London Dyers and Cleaners for over 120 years (cleaners
   of everything for everyone)
P/Eastman/SG
Dyers of High Degree
P/Eastman/V&A records
The Westminster Press
P/WP/*Comm Art* vol 1 1926 p 71
Pomeroy Day Cream
P/Pomeroy/SG, V&A
He who gets slapped
P/Theater Guild NYC/*Comm Art* Dec 1923 p 326
Back to Methuselah. Four hand-lettered posters
P/Theater Guild NYC/SG
Back to Methuselah
P/Theater Guild NYC/SG
SS Tenacity
P/Shubert Theater Corp/press cutting, Evansville Mus of
   Arts and Science, June 8 1922
The Dover Road
P/Shubert Theater Corp/press cutting, Evansville Mus of
   Science and Art
Samuel Pepys Esq by E. Hallam Moorhouse
Bj/Leonard Parsons/SG

1923

London Dyers and Cleaners for over 120 years
P/Eastman/V&A
London Dyers and Cleaners for over 100 years
P/Eastman/SG
Pomeroy Day Cream
P/Pomeroy/V&A
ALS Travelling theatre at Royal Court Theatre
P/ALS/coll M.B. Zimmern, London
Read Cricketer in the *Manchester Guardian*
P/MG/British Council (Alan Mabey coll)
Vim
P/Lever Bros/SG
Since 1802. The London Dyers and Cleaners
P/Eastman/V&A
Regatta time at Molesey
P?/Tramways/*Comm Art* Sept 1923 (possibly not issued)
Woman – a vindication by Anthony Ludovici
Bj/Constable/SG
Peace in our time by Oliver Onions
Bj/Chapman and Hall/SG
Babel by John Cournos
Bj/Heinemann/SG

1924

Winter Sales are best reached by Underground
P/UD/V&A, MMA
The Vindictive Howitzer – IWM
P/UD/V&A, MMA, V&A (od)
Olympia Show
P/UD/LT
Museum of Natural History
P/UD/V&A
The Colne River at Uxbridge by Tram
P/UD/V&A, LoC
Twickenham by Tram
P/UD/V&A, LoC
Hadley Wood by Tram
P/UD/V&A, MMA, LoC
Near Waltham Cross by Tram
P/UD/V&A, V&A (od)
Bushey Park by Tram
P/UD/V&A
Spring cleaning
P/Eastman/V&A
The Arts League travelling theatre, the travelling players
   are coming
P/ALS/private coll, London
Eight posters for the British Empire exhibition of 1924.
   Food, Chemistry, Sport, Home-making, Electricity,
   Pottery, Mining, Theatres
P/BEE/L. Weaver, *Exhibitions and the arts of display*,
   London 1925 figs 361, 362 & 365
Eno's Fruit Salt – first thing every morning (crowing
   cock)
P/Eno/V&A, MMA
note: also used as Pa
Eno's Fruit Salt – first thing every morning (cock on
   weather-vane)
P/Eno/AMB
The Week-end Book: A Sociable Anthology
Bj/Nonesuch/SG
Books and Characters by Lytton Strachey
Bj/C&W/SG
Queen Victoria by Lytton Strachey
Bj/C&W/SG

1925

The Wallace Collection
P/UD/V&A, V&A (od)
The Indian Museum, Imperial Institute
P/UD/V&A
Whitsuntide border design & headpiece
P/UD/LT
The new aquarium at the Zoo
P?/UD/*Vogue* May 1925 (possibly not used)
Summertime in the country
P/UD/V&A
Summertime pleasures by Underground (pierrot)
P/UD/V&A, MMA
Summertime pleasures by Underground (jack in the
   green)
P/UD/V&A, MMA
note: this design and the previous two entries were also
   issued with the alternative wording 'Whitsuntide'
England to India/A World record in a Wolseley
P/Wolseley/CHM
The new trade-mark of Eastman and Sons
P/Eastman/V&A
Spring cleaning and dyeing
P/Eastman/V&A
London Group RWS Galleries
P/LG/V&A, MMA
Welwyn Garden City, less than an hour from Piccadilly
   Circus. A town that is planned, a home to be proud of
P/Welwyn Garden Estates Office/British Council (Alan
   Mabey coll)
The Labour Woman
P/Labour Woman/MMA
Expressionism by Hermann Bahr
Bj/F Henderson/CHM
That fool of a woman by Millicent, Duchess of Sutherland
Bj/Putnam/*Comm Art* 1927 p 107
The Anatomy of Melancholy by Richard Burton. 150 line
   ills, Nonesuch press, London 4to. 2 vols, 750 sets. 40
   copies on japon vellum with line ills hand-coloured by
   the Curwen Press. See Francis Meynell, *The Nonesuch
   Century*, London 1930
Bi

1926

The flea at the Natural History Museum
P/UD/V&A, MMA, V&A (od)
Socrates at the British Museum
P/UD/MMA
Eastman and Son since 1802
P/Eastman/*Comm Art Annual*, Posters & Publicity, 1927
    p 123
Gloves Cleaned
P/Eastman/MMA, *Gebrauchsgraphik* May 1929 p 40
Pomeroy Skin Food
P/Pomeroy/*Comm Art* vol 1 1926 p 70
One third of the Empire is in the tropics. 3 illustrative
    posters (Cocoa Pods, Growing markets for our goods, &
    Bananas) and 2 typographic designs
P/Empire/Cocoa Pods, MMA, Northampton College of
    Art, V&A (od). Bananas, MMA ill in *Comm Art* New
    Series vol 4, 1928 p 45
Ivor Novello in *The Lodger*
P/Gainsborough Pictures/MMA (od)
Metropolis
P/client unknown/MMA (od)
Benito Cereno by Herman Melville. Nonesuch Fo. 1650
    copies printed at Curwen Press. Letterpress ills with
    stencilled water-colour
Bi
The Clio by L.H. Myers
Bj/client unknown/*Comm Art* 1927 p 105
The Lodger
Bj/client unknown/

1927

From Winter's gloom to Summer's joy
P/UD/MMA, V&A
Publicity
P/UD/LT
Cheap Return Tickets, 4 versions
P/UD/LT
Hearts and Diamonds
P/client unknown/*Comm Art* July 1927 p 101
Today's pick of the Empire Basket
P/Empire/V&A (od)
Bass
P/Bass/*Comm Art* vol 5 1928 p 106
Who's for Bass?
P/Bass/*Comm Art* vol 5 1928 p 106
Raising Standards to increase Sales
Bj/Adelphi Assoc/*Comm Art Annual*, Posters and
    Publicity, 1927
Modern Movements in Art by R.H. Wilenski
Bj/Faber & Gwyer/SG
England reclaimed by Osbert Sitwell
Bj/Duckworth/V&A
Giants in the Earth by O.E. Rølvaag
Bj/Harper & Bros/*Gebrauchsgraphik* May 1929 p 43
Shaken by the wind by Ray Strachey
Bj/Faber & Gwyer/*Gebrauchsgraphik* May 1929 p 43
Pilgrims by Ethel Mannin
Bj/Jarrolds/SG
'Journey of the Magi' by T.S. Eliot (Ariel poem no 8)
Bj/Faber & Gwyer/V&A

1928

Articas Britanicos
P/Client unknown/Sir Joseph Duveen, *30 years of British
    Art*, London 1930 p 3
Chrysler prices are down
P/Chrysler Motors Ltd/MMA
Brook Evans by Susan Glaspell
Bj/Gollancz/Gollancz (od)
Words and Music by George Rylands
Bj/L & V Woolf
Cornelian by Harold Acton
Bj/C&W/CHM, SG
Departure by Roland Dorgeles
Bj/Gollancz/*Gebrauchsgraphik* May 1929 p 43
Mystery at Lynden Sands by J.J. Connington
Bj/Gollancz/*Gebrauchsgraphik* May 1929 p 43

Lord Peter views the body by Dorothy L. Sayers
Bj/Gollancz/Sheila Hodges, *Gollancz*, London 1978 p 33
2LO, A Detective story by Walter S. Masterman
Bj/Gollancz/*Gebrauchsgraphik* ay 1929 p 43
The Bleston Mystery by Robert Milward Kennedy
Bj/Gollancz/*Gebrauchsgraphik* May 1929 p 43
The Golem by Gustav Meyrink
Bj/Gollancz/*Gebrauchsgraphik* May 1929 p 43
The unholy three by Tod Robbins
Bj/Gollancz/SG
'A Song for Simeon' by T.S. Eliot (Ariel poem no 16)
Bi/Faber & Gwyer/V&A

1929

St Albans Route 84
P/UD/LT
Exhibition of Native Art from British Columbia
P/UD/MMA
Olympia Show
P/UD/*Architectural Review* vol 65 p 221
International Aero exhibition
P/Shell/V&A, BP archives (no 213)
Well Done! 11 World Records
P/Villiers/CHM, MMA
BBC Handbook for 1929
Bj/BBC/BBC archives
Imperialism and the open conspiracy by H.G. Wells
Bj/Faber & Faber/SG
Robinson Crusoe by Daniel Defoe. Etchells and Macdonald.
    4to 535 copies, 7 ills litho key with stencilled gouache
    by the Curwen Press
Bi
Elsie and the Child by Arnold Bennett. Cassell & Co. 8vo.
    750 copies, 9 ills and vignette stencilled in gouache
    over litho key by the Curwen Press
Bi
note: binding design also by Kauffer

20s

The Last Revelation by Adagea
Bj/client unknown/SG
The Island of Captain Sparrow by S. Fowler Wright
Bj/client unknown/SG

1930

Play between 6 & 12, the bright hours
P/UD/V&A
Shop between 10 & 4, the quiet hours
P/UD/V&A, MMA
Power, the nerve centre of London's Underground
P/UD/V&A, MMA
For all theatres, travel Underground
P/UD/V&A, MMA, V&A (od, alternative version)
For pull use Summer Shell
P/Shell/V&A, BP, MMA
Modern Jewelry by Raymond Templier
P/Curtis Moffat/CHM records
Players Please
P/W.D. & H.O. Wills/CHM records
Marina by T.S. Eliot (Ariel poem no 29)
Bj/Faber & Gwyer/V&A
The Fiery Angel by Valeri Bryusov
Bj/H. Toulmin/SG
Don Quixote by Miguel de Cervantes. The Nonesuch
    Press. 8yo. 2 vols 1475 sets. Text printed at C U P, 21
    ills printed at the Curwen Press by photogravure and
    stencilled water-colour
Bi/Nonesuch/V&A
The World in 2030 AD by Frederick Edwin Smith, first
    Earl of Birkenhead
Bi/Hodder and Stoughton/CHM

1931

Michael Faraday Centenary Exhibition
P/UD/MMA
Underground Progress
P/UD/LT

You can be sure of Shell (Chain)
Lb/Shell/BP/MMA
See Britain first on Shell – Stonehenge
Lb/Shell/V&A, MMA
New Forest, See Britain first on Shell
Lb/Shell/V&A, MMA
The Quick starting pair
Lb/Shell/SG, BP
Recommendation Chart
P/Shell/BP
Austin Reed
P/AR/coll Ken Russell, Borrowdale (od)
no printed example known
Venus rising from the sea by Arnold Bennett. Cassell & Co.
    8vo. 350 copies. 13 ills hand stencilled in water-colour
    over litho key by the Curwen Press
Bi/Cassell/V&A
Triumphal March by T.S. Eliot
Bi/Faber & Faber/V&A

1932

Look! Under that broad beech tree . . . (Walton)
P/Underground/V&A
A Pillar'd shade . . . (Milton)
P/UD/V&A, LoC
By the rushy-fringed bank . . . (Milton)
P/UD/V&A, LoC, MMA
Now the pine-tree's waving top . . . (Cunningham)
P/UD/V&A, LoC
Publicity pays on the Underground
P/Underground/MMA
Piccadilly Express Trains
P/UD/LT
note: also issued as a car panel
Bodiam Castle
Lb/Shell/BP, MMA
Economise in time, temper, petrol
Lb/Shell/MMA, BP
The River Yeo near Barnstaple
Lb/Shell/BP, MMA
Aeroshell lubricating oil
Lb/Shell/BP, MMA, V&A
Go Great Western to Devonshire
P/GWR(no 10)/V&A, MMA
Go Great Western to Devon
P/GWR(no 11)/CHM, V&A
Go Great Western to Devon's Moors
P/GWR(no 12)/V&A/MMA
Great Western to Cornwall
P/GWR(no 13)/MMA/V&A
Go Great Western to Cornwall
P/GWR(no 14)/MMA/V&A
Go Great Western to Cornwall
P/GWR(no 15)/V&A, MMA
Lewis Carroll Centenary
P/J. & E. Bumpus/CHM
Murder on the Yacht by Rufus King
Bj/Doubleday Doran/SG
The Greater Britain by Oswald Mosley
Bj/British Union of Fascists/SG
Glorious Devon by S.P.B. Mais
Bj/GWR/V&A
The Cornish Riviera by S.P.B. Mais
Bj/GWR/V&A

1933

Whitsuntide Holiday, Off to the country
P/LPTB/SG, LoC, CHM, MMA
Ask for 'BP' Ethyl
Lb/Shell/SG, MMA
Aladdin, the best paraffin, coloured pink for your
    protection
Lb/Shell/SG, BP
Merchants prefer Shell
Lb/Shell/MMA/BP
Recommended for Winter – Double Shell lubricating Oil
P/Shell/SG, MMA
Horse-Power BP Ethyl Anti-Knock
Lb/Shell/V&A, MMA
note: also issued as a 48-sheet poster and car panel
Gilbey's Castle Port
P/WAG/V&A, MMA

Rubicon Burgundy
P/WAG/V&A, MMA
W & A Gilbey Ltd Wines and Spirits
P/WAG/V&A, MMA
Gilbey's Invalid Port
P/WAG/V&A, MMA
Gilbey's Invalid Port
P/WAG/MMA
Wrangoo Australian Red Wine
P/WAG/MMA
Spey Royal Scotch Whiskey
P/WAG/MMA, V&A
Bonita Sherry
P/WAG/V&A
Ask for 404 Bincoln Lennett's latest
P/Lincoln Bennett/SG
Singing out of tune by Brian Guinness
Bj/Putnam/SG
Patriotism Ltd . . . the exposure of the war machine
Bj/Union of Democratic Control/SG
Art Now by Herbert Read
Bj/Faber & Faber/SG
note: binding also designed by Kauffer (V&A)

1934

Pyramid Handkerchiefs
P/client unknown/SG (od), no printed example known
7-day season – holidays in the West Country
P/GWR/MMA
At London's service. Two versions/St Paul's, The Tower,
    Roman bath, Palace of Westminster,/National Portrait
    Gallery, Banqueting House, British Museum, The
    Tower
P/LPTB/SG
Buckingham Palace
P/LPTB/V&A, MMA, LoC
Westminster Abbey
P/LPTB/V&A, MMA
The Tower of London
P/LPTB/V&A, MMA
Westminster from the Thames
P/LPTB/V&A, SG, MMA, LoC
Publicity pays the World
P/LPTB/MMA, LT
Magicians prefer Shell
Lb/Shell/V&A, MMA
Explorers prefer Shell
Lb/Shell/SG, MMA
Contact the World. Use the Telephone
P/GPO/SG, MMA
Come on the telephone
P/GPO/MMA
Orient Line Cruises 1934
P/Orient/V&A
Ships and Services
P/Orient/CHM records
Keep well. Eno's fruit salt. First thing every morning
P/Eno/SG
Regent Exhibition of 1934, Dorland Hall
P/client unknown/MMA
Landscape with figures by Brian Guinness
Bj/Putnam/coll Lord Moyne
The Maltese Falcon by Dashiell Hammett
Bj/Modern Library/CHM

1935

Toys. Three posters advertising public collections
P/LPTB/V&A
Train yourself for better work
P/LPTB/SG, MMA
Treat yourself to better play
P/LPTB/V&A, SG, MMA
Evening classes, Surrey area
P/LPTB/MMA
Education
P/LPTB/V&A exhib cat 1955 no 27, listed as a
    companion to the previous two posters
Shell is always first
Lb/Shell/SG, MMA
Winter Shell – On sale till next May
Lb/Shell/MMA
Royal Windsor
P/GWR/LT
Air Mail Routes
P/GPO/SG
Quickest by Air Mail
P/GPO/MMA

Orient Line to Australia and back. £140 first class
P/Orient/CHM, MMA, LoC
Stephens Ink
P/Stephens Ink/SG (od), no printed example known
Travel in comfort by Imperial Airways. Europe, Africa,
    India and the East
P/Imperial/SG, MMA
The new gas fires light themselves says Dr Therm
P/Gas, Light & Coke Co/SG, MMA
Stop on India non-skid tyres . . .
P/India/SG
Things to come by H.G. Wells
Bj/Cresset Press/SG
5 on Revolutionary Art
Bj/Wishart/SG
Quack Quack by Leonard Woolf
Bj/Hogarth Press/SG

1936

Special Areas Exhibition, Charing Cross Station
P/LPTB/CHM, MMA
The Empire's Airways Exhibition, Science Museum
P/LPTB/LT
Four posters on the theme of 'Spring'; Spring on the hill-
    siie (photo by J Dixon-Scott)/Spring in the Village
    (photo by Kate Jacob)/Follow the Spring, Ripley (photo
    by Paul Shillabeer)/Follow the Spring, Shardeloes
    Park, (photo by Paul Shillabeer)
P/LPTB/*Art & Industry*, vol 22 1937 p 176, SG
Earl's Court. See the model of the new building
P/LPTB/MMA, V&A
Official for Winter, Double Shell
Lb/Shell/MMA, *Modern Publicity* 1937–8 p 21
Ford approve Triple Shell
P/Shell/BP
Morris recommend
P/Shell/BP
Single Shell, Hillman, Rolls-Royce, Standard
P/Shell/BP
Dinton Castle near Aylesbury
P/Shell/V&A, MMA
London can double its Winter sunshine. Use gas and
    coke, fire without smoke
P/Gas, Light and Coke Co/V&A (od)
Help wounded human beings. Help to send medical aid to
    Spain
P/SMAC/MMA, AMB
Tea drives away the droops says Mr T Pott (photo of
    Gracie Fields)
P/Client unknown/SG
Batsford Pictorial Guides: no 1 Amsterdam
Bj/Batsford/V&A
Strange Glory by L.H. Myers
Bj/Putnam/coll John Byrne, London
The man who could work miracles by H.G. Wells
Bj/Cresset Press/SG
Henry Esmond by William M. Thackeray
Bj/Modern Library/CHM

1937

It's not far to the new Earl's Court (with six different
    station names overprinted)
P/LPTB/SG
August Bank Holiday out by LT
P/LPTB/CHM
Earl's Court Motor Show
P/LT/LT
Spring. Easter in the country
P/LPTB/SG
Spring. 'Still the fresh spring . . .'
P/LPTB/V&A
Lubrication by Shell – Miles Whitney-Straight Aeroplane
Lb/Shell/MMA
Lubricate by Shell. Imperial Flying Boat Canopus
Lb/Shell/BP, MMA
Cheaper Empire Telegrams
P/GPO/GPO (od)
Outposts of Britain: Land's End
P/GPO/GPO (od)
Outposts of Britain: Northern Ireland
P/GPO/GPO
Outposts of Britain: The Pool of London
P/GPO/CHM, SG, GPO (od)
Outposts of Britain: The North of Scotland
P/GPO/CHM, GPO (od)

Post during the lunch hour
P/GPO/SG, MMA
Letter Mails by Air to East & South Africa. Egypt,
    Palestine, India, Ceylon, Burma, Malaya. 1½d for each
    ½oz. Post cards one penny.
P/GPO/SG, MMA, *Penrose Annual* vol 41 1939 p 24, LoC,
    GPO (od)
Millions can save, save, save
P/GPO/CHM records
Post Office savings bank
P/GPO/MMA
News Chronicle Schools Exhibition, Dorland Hall
P/*News Chronicle*/MMA
New Architecture exhibition of the elements of modern
    architecture organised by the MARS group
P/MARS/SG
Use your Health services
P/Min of Health/V&A
Study Success at the Advertising Exhibition Olympia
P/Advertising Exhibition/SG, CHM, MMA
Continual Dew by John Betjeman
Bj/John Murray/CHM
Smoky Crusade by R.M. Fox
Bj/The Hogarth Press/coll John Byrne, London
Checkmate score by Arthur Bliss
Bj/Boosey & Hawkes/SG

1938

A Summer landscape (fields)
P/LPTB/V&A, *Architectural Review* 1949 p 254, LoC
Autumn Woods
P/LT/V&A, LoC
note: reissued by LT in 1955 lettered 'How bravely
    Autumn paints upon the Sky' (Hood). V&A, LoC
Shell turns the wheels of the World
P/Shell/V&A, *Modern Publicity* 1939–40 p 31
T V O Tractor Vaporising Oil, for maximum draw-bar
    pull!
Lb/Shell/BP, V&A, MMA
Shell for go for Shell
Lb/Shell/BP, MMA
National Volunteers Service. Wanted for Women's
    Ambulance Services ARP3
P/ARP/SG
Air Raid Precautions calling You
P/ARP/V&A, CHM, MMA
Exhibition of Chinese Art
P/Chinese Medical Aid/SG
Support the National Memorial Fund (for the British
    Battalion)
P/Dependant and Wounded Committee/MMA
Support the International Brigade
P/Client unknown/CHM
Webster Aitken playing Schubert's complete pianoforte
    sonatas
P/Aeolian Hall/SG, MMA
Films/Art/Music/Entertainment/Fame for Britain
P/Client unknown/V&A
Festival of music for the people. Royal Albert Hall,
    Conway Hall, Queens Hall
P/Client unknown/SG
News Chronicle Schools Exhibition at the Dorland Hall
P/*News Chronicle*/MMA
The man below by H.T. Hopkinson
Bj/The Hogarth Press/coll John Byrne, London
Lions and Shadows by Christopher Isherwood
Bi/The Hogarth Press/CHM (5 spot ills, perhaps from
    magazine)

1939

London Music Festival April 23–May 28
P/LT/LT
Natural History Museum
P/LT/V&A
note: this design reached proof stage but was not issued
    because of WWII. Finally issued by LT in 1974. V&A
Summer Shell May to October
P/Shell/V&A, MMA, BP
Winter Shell October–May
P/Shell/V&A, BP
National Volunteers Service
P/ARP/British Council (coll Alan Mabey)
International Brigade
P/British War relief/CHM

30S

South and East African Air Mail make every day posting
day
P/GPO/MMA
Power
Sh/Shell/SG
Billy Budd by Herman Melville. First mentioned as
designed by Kauffer in *Who's Who* 1931 and in
subsequent reference books. Not known
Bi

1940

Lend to defend the right to be free
P/Min of Information/V&A (od), no printed example
known
Together Victory
P/Min of Information/V&A (od), no printed example
known
Lincoln Continental for 1941
P/Ford Motor Co/*20th Annual of Advertising Art*, Art
Directors' Club of NY 1941 p 200
Life of Timon of Athens by William Shakespeare
Bi/Limited Editions Club NY/CHM (od), not used
Don Quixote by Miguel de Cervantes
Bj/Modern Library/SG
Maigret travels South by Georges Simenon
Bj/Harcourt Brace/CHM
Drink to yesterday by Manning Coles
Bj/Alfred A. Knopf/CHM
Europe in Spring by Clare Boothe
Bj/Alfred A. Knopf/CHM
Journey into fear by Eric Ambler
Bj/Alfred A. Knopf/CHM
Dracula by Bram Stoker
Bj/Modern Library/CHM
The sun also rises by Ernest Hemingway
Bj/Modern Library/CHM
Sanctuary by William Faulkner
Bj/Modern Library/CHM
The portrait of a lady by Henry James
Bj/Modern Library/CHM
The Life of Michelangelo by John Addington Symonds
Bj/Modern Library/V&A, CHM
The Old Wives' Tale by Arnold Bennett
Bj/Modern Library/CHM
Seven Mysteries of Europe by Jules Romains
Bj/Alfred A. Knopf/CHM

1941

CIO supports Red Cross
P/National CIO War Relief Committee/CHM
Squadrons Up by Noel Monks
Bj/Macgraw-Hill/CHM
A Sentimental Journey by Laurence Sterne
Bj/Modern Library/CHM
Tristram Shandy by Laurence Sterne
Bj/Modern Library/CHM
Gargantua and Pantagruel, by Rabelais
Bj/Modern Library/*Modern Artist* April 1941
I saw England by Ben Robertson
Bj/Alfred A. Knopf/CHM
The Astors by Harvey O'Connor
Bj/Alfred A. Knopf/CHM

1942

The greatest show on Earth
P/Ringling/CHM
Greece fights on
P/Greek Office of Information/SG, MMA, LoC
El Nuevo Orden . . . del Eje
P/Publicado/CHM, LoC
Libertad de Cultos
P/Publicado/CHM
Luchamos por la libertad de Todas
P/Publicado/CHM, LoC
This was Cicero by H.J. Haskell
Bj/Alfred A. Knopf/CHM

The Widening Stain by W. Bolingbroke Johnson
Bj/Alfred A. Knopf/CHM
The book of modern composers ed. David Ewen
Bj/Alfred A. Knopf/CHM
News is a weapon by Matthew Gordon
Bj/Alfred A. Knopf/CHM
When last I died by Gladys Mitchell
Bj/Alfred A. Knopf/CHM
Disraeli by André Maurois
Bj/Modern Library/CHM
Hangover Square by Patrick Hamilton
Bj/Random House/CHM
Three famous spy novels by Bennett A. Cerf
Bj/Random House/CHM
The setting sun of Japan by Carl Randan and Leane
Zugsmith
Bj/Random House/CHM
Farewell pretty ladies by Chris Massie
Bj/Random House/CHM
The way of all flesh by Samuel Butler
Bj/World Publications/CHM
Faust by Wolfgang von Goethe
Bj/World Publications/CHM
The film sense by Serge Eisenstein
Bj/Harcourt Brace/CHM
Shakespeare in Harlem by Langston Hughes
Bi/Alfred A. Knopf/CHM

1943

Holidays
P/Ringling/CHM
Norway fights on
P/American friends of Norway/CHM
Target No. 1 – New York City
P/Office of Civilian Defence/CHM
Watch out for fires
P/CAA War training Service/CHM, LoC
Steel! not bread
P/US War Bond Drive/CHM, Baltimore Mus of Art (od)
Help a Greek child to survive
P/Friends of Greece Inc/CHM
XAIRETE NIKOMEN
P/Greek War relief assoc/CHM, MMA, IWM, LoC
Rebecca by Daphne du Maurier
Bj/Modern Library/CHM
Clausewitz on war trans. J. Matthijs Jolles
Bj/Modern Library/CHM
Man the measure by Erich Kähler
Bj/Pantheon/CHM
The Dream Department by S.J. Perelman
Bj/Random House/CHM
Makers of Modern Strategy by Edward Mead Earle
Bj/Princeton Univ Press/CHM
The Arabs by Philip K. Hitti
Bj/Princeton Univ Press/CHM
The struggle for airways in Latin America by William A.M.
Burden
Bj/Council on Foreign Relations/CHM
Poems by Dunstan Thompson
Bj/Simon and Schuster/CHM
The people from heaven by John Sanford
Bj/Harcourt Brace/CHM
The wide net by Eudora Welty
Bj/Harcourt Brace/CHM
Three of a kind by James A. Kane
Bj/Alfred A. Knopf/CHM
Chicago Blueprints by John L. Balderston
Bj/Alfred A. Knopf/CHM
These are the Generals by Walter A. Mills
Bj/Alfred A. Knopf/CHM

1944

Yugoslav people led by Tito, 1941–1944
P/UCSSA/CHM, LoC
Drainy Weather, Conoco the Motor Oil
P/Continental Oil Co/*24th Art Directors' Annual of
Advertising Art* 1945 p 274
Moby Dick by Herman Melville
Bj/Modern Library/CHM
Now is Mexico by Hudson Strode
Bj/Harcourt Brace/CHM

Palgrave's Golden Treasury
Bj/Modern Library/CHM
Famous Ghost Stories by Bennett A. Cerf
Bj/Random House/CHM
Per Ardua by Hilary St George Saunders
Bj/Oxford University Press/CHM
Beast in view by Muriel Rukeyser
Bj/Doubleday Doran/CHM
Halfway House by Ellery Queen
Bj/Pocket Books/CHM
Green Mansions by W.H. Hudson, Random House. 8vo.
Unlimited edition. 31 illus, 9 in col, by offset
lithography
Bi/Random House/V&A

1945

Give
P/American Red Cross/CHM, (postcard version)
Hunger on Wheels
P/N Y Subways Advertising Co/CHM
Join the Diamond Jubilee
P/Metropolitan Museum of Art/CHM
The Rainbow to Europe. Tourist fares $270 one
way/$486 return
P/Pan Am/CHM
The Death of Virgil (and German edition, *Der Tod de Vergil*)
Bj/Pantheon/CHM
Foundations of National Power by Harold and Margaret
Sprout
Bj/Princeton Univ Press/CHM
The Children of Wrath by Glenro Wescott
Bj/Harpers & Bros/CHM
Challenge at Chagsa by Paul Hughes
Bj/Macmillan/CHM
Mainsprings of Civilisation by Ellesworth Huntington
Bj/J. Wiley & Sons/CHM
Elizabeth is missing by Lillian de la Torre
Bj/Alfred A. Knopf/CHM

1946

Stranger than truth by Vera Caspary
Bj/Random House/CHM
Brewsie and Willie by Gertrude Stein
Bj/Random House/CHM
You and the Universe by John J. O'Neill
Bj/I Washburn/CHM
The price of Liberty by Maikia Pezas
Bj/Gollancz/CHM
The Faith of a Liberal by Morris R. Cohen
Bj/Henry Holt/CHM
The path of Science by Kenneth Mees
Bj/J. Wiley & Sons/CHM
The complete poems and stories of Edgar Allan Poe. Alfred A.
Knopf. 8vo. 2 vols. Unlimited edition. 39 illustrations
Bi/Knopf/V&A

1947

United Nations: your peace is our business
P/United Nations/*Art & Industry* vol 43 Oct 1947 p 119
American Airlines over the World
P/American Airlines/CHM
Subway posters perform daily before 5 million pairs of
eyes (no 1)
P/N Y Subway Advertising Co/CHM, AMB
note: also issued as a mailing piece and magazine
advertisement
When the mountain fell by C.F. Ramuz
Bj/Pantheon/CHM
The Sleep Walkers by Herman Broch
Bj/Pantheon/CHM
Roseanna McCoy by Alberta Hannum
Bj/Henry Holt/CHM
The prodigal never returns by Hugh Chisholm
Bj/Farrar, Straus/CHM
Pre-historic pottery in Egypt by Max Raphael
Bj/Pantheon/CHM
The Landslide by C.F. Ramuz
Bj/Pantheon/CHM

1948

The Tourist
P/American Airlines/V&A 1955 Exhib Cat no 25
San Francisco
P/American Airlines/MMA
American Airlines to New England
P/American Airlines/CHM
American Airlines/All Europe
P/American Airlines/CHM
Washington/American Airlines
P/American Airlines/CHM, LoC
American Airlines to Europe
P/American Airlines/CHM, MMA
American Airlines/Scandinavia
P/American Airlines/CHM
American Airlines/California/Arizona/Texas/New
  Mexico
P/American Airlines/LoC, 30th Art Directors' Annual
  1951 p 223
American Airlines to Mexico
P/American Airlines/CHM, LoC
Fashions in Flight via American Airlines
P/American Airlines/CHM, LoC
American Airlines/Mexico
P/American Airlines/CHM
American Airlines
P/American Airlines/CHM
American Airlines to California
P/American Airlines/CHM, LoC
American Airlines to Washington/Night & Day
P/American Airlines/CHM
American Airlines to Ireland
P/American Airlines/CHM
Holland
P/American Airlines/CHM, V&A
American Airlines to England
P/American Airlines/CHM, V&A
American Airlines/Washington/Baltimore/New York/
  Boston/New England/East Coast
P/American Airlines/CHM, LoC
American Airlines/California/Switzerland/Canada/
  Scandinavia/New England
P/American Airlines/CHM
American Airlines/San Francisco
P/American Airlines/CHM, LoC
To Niagara Falls & Canada
P/American Airlines/CHM
Winter Sports
P/American Airlines/CHM
To New York
P/American Airlines/CHM, LoC
Germany/Fly Pan American/World's most experienced
  airline
P/Pan Am/CHM
Egyptian Servant Statues by James H. Breasted Jnr
Bj/Pantheon/CHM
The limits of Art by Huntington Cairns
Bj/Pantheon/CHM
The King and the Corpse by Heinrich Zimmer
Bj/Pantheon/CHM
Psychic energy by M. Esther Harding
Bj/Pantheon/CHM
Latin America by Ray Josephs
Bj/Random House/CHM
Intruder in the dust by William Faulkner
Bj/Random House/CHM ,
From Poe to Valery by T.S. Eliot
Bj/Harcourt Brace/CHM
A Clouded star by Anne Parrish
Bj/Harper & Bros/CHM
Indonesian Art by R. von Heine-Gelden
Bj/Asia Institute (NY)/CHM
Art Now by Herbert Read
Bj/Faber & Faber/CHM
On the Iliad by Rachel Bespaloff
Bj/Pantheon/CHM

1949

Subway Poster Pulls (no 9)
P/N Y Subway Advertising Co/CHM
28th National Exhibition of Advertising and Editorial Art
P/MMA/CHM
For quick results – ship by clipper cargo
P/Pan Am/CHM
Mexico. Festivals Old & New. Pan American the World's
  most experienced airline
P/Pan Am/V&A, CHM

Secret Valleys by John Cousins
Bj/Alfred A. Knopf/CHM
The hero with a thousand faces by Joseph Campbell
Bj/Pantheon/CHM
Essays on a science of mythology by C.J. Jung & C. Kerenyi
Bj/Pantheon/CHM
Wicked water by Mackinley Kantor
Bj/Random House/CHM
Exile by St John Perse
Bj/Pantheon/CHM

40S

28th Annual Exhibition of Advertising and Editorial Art
P/MMA/CHM
He wants to know – keep it under your stetson
P/Client unknown/coll L. Rackow, New York City
Civil Aeronautics Administration
P/CAA/MMA
Point counter point by Aldous Huxley
Bj/Modern Library/SG
The Medici by C.F. Young
Bj/Modern Library/SG
Nigger Heaven by Carl van Vechten
Bi/Client unknown/MMA (od)

1950

Chicago
P/American Airlines/V&A
Kentucky Derby May 7. Go via Chesapeake & Ohio
P/Chesapeake & Ohio railroad/V&A
Holy Year. Rome 1950 American Airlines
P/American Airlines/CHM
American Airlines. Paris
P/American Airlines/CHM
American Airlines/Sweden
P/American Airlines/V&A, CHM
The Hieroglyphics of Horapollo by George Boas
Bj/Pantheon/CHM
The Dream of Poliphilo by Linda Fierz-David
Bj/Pantheon/CHM
Navaho religion by Gladys A. Reichard
Bj/Pantheon/CHM
Religion and the cure of souls in Jung's psychology by Hans
  Schaer
Bj/Pantheon/CHM
The I ching by Wilheim C.F. Baynes
Bj/Pantheon/CHM
Tristram Shandy by Laurence Sterne
Bj/Modern Library/CHM
Light in August by William Faulkner
Bj/Modern Library/CHM

1951

No work recorded this year

1952

African Folktales and Sculpture by Paul Radin & Elino
  Marrel
Bj/Pantheon/CHM

1953

To Boston
P/American Airlines/CHM
Round the World. Fly with Pan American
P/Pan Am/V&A
Aloha Hawaii
P/Pan Am/CHM, V&A, LoC
Ireland. Fly Pan Am
P/Pan Am/CHM
The Decameron by Boccaccio
Bj/Modern Library/CHM

1954

Japan via Pan American
P/Pan Am/V&A
Mademoiselle de Maupin by Théophile Gautier
Bj/Modern Library/CHM
The Fables of La Fontaine by Marianne Moore
Bj/Viking Press/coll Grace Schulman, NYC

Index